TECHNOLOGY IN ANCIENT CULTURES

ANCIENT CONSTRUCTION TECHNOLOGY

FROM PYRAMIDS TO FORTRESSES

Michael Woods and
Mary B. Woods

Twenty-First Century Books · Minneapolis

To Alexander and Caden Woods

Twenty-First Century Books
A division of Lerner Publishing Group, Inc.
241 First Avenue North
Minneapolis, MN 55401 U.S.A.

Website address: www.lernerbooks.com

Library of Congress Cataloging-in-Publication Data

Woods, Michael, 1946–
  Ancient construction technology : from pyramids to fortresses / by Michael Woods and Mary
 B. Woods.
      p.   cm. – (Technology in ancient cultures)
   Includes bibliographical references and index.
   ISBN 978-0-7613-6527-3 (lib. bdg. : alk. paper)
   1. Building—History—To 1500—Juvenile literature. 2. Antiquities—Juvenile literature. I. Woods, Mary
 B. (Mary Boyle), 1946– II. Title.
  TH16.W66 2011
  690.093—dc22   2010025582

Manufactured in the United States of America
1 – PC – 12/31/10

TABLE OF CONTENTS

THE ANCIENT WORLDS OF CONSTRUCTION

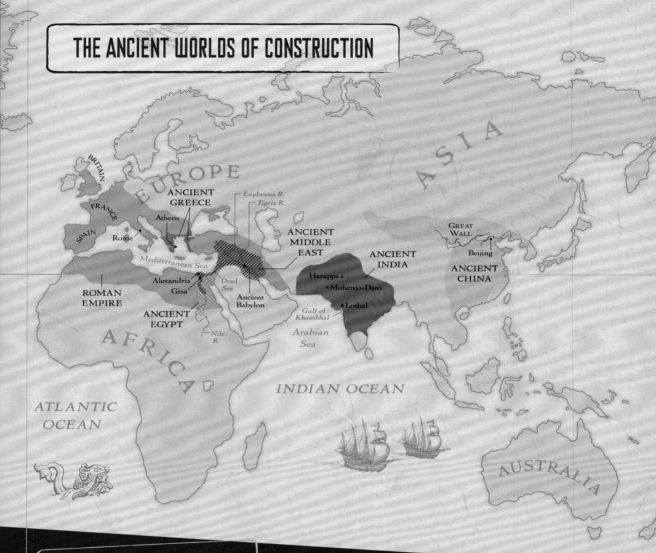

BRITAIN

EUROPE

ASIA

FRANCE

ANCIENT
GREECE

Euphrates R.
Tigris R.

SPAIN

Athens

Rome

ANCIENT
MIDDLE
EAST

GREAT
WALL

ANCIENT
INDIA

Beijing

ANCIENT
CHINA

Mediterranean Sea

ROMAN
EMPIRE

Alexandria
Giza

Dead
Sea

Harappa
Mohenjo-Daro

Ancient
Babylon

Lothal

ANCIENT
EGYPT

Gulf of
Khambhal

AFRICA

Nile
R.

Arabian
Sea

ATLANTIC
OCEAN

INDIAN OCEAN

AUSTRALIA

INTRODUCTION

What do you think of when you hear the word *technology*? You probably think of something totally new. You might think of research laboratories filled with computers, powerful microscopes, and other scientific tools. But technology doesn't mean just brand-new machines and discoveries. Technology is as old as human civilization.

Technology is the use of knowledge, inventions, and discoveries to make life better. The word *technology* comes from two Greek words. One, *techne*, means "art" or "craft." The other, *logos*, means "logic" or "reason." In ancient Greece, the word *technology* meant a discussion of arts and crafts. In modern times, technology usually refers to the craft, the technique, or the tool itself.

▲ Mohenjo Daro, in modern-day Pakistan, was once home to thousands of people. Archaeologists study the ruins of the city to learn about ancient construction.

People use many kinds of technology. Transportation is one kind of technology. Medicine and agriculture are also technologies. These technologies and many others can make life easier, safer, and more enjoyable. This book looks at a form of technology that fulfills the basic human need for shelter: construction.

FROM THE GROUND UP

The story of construction is the story of human society. The first humans on Earth moved from place to place, looking for fresh sources of food. They often built new shelters every time they moved. Their building technology was simple. They used poles and animal skins to make tents. They wove reeds together to make huts. A tree trunk laid across a stream was the first bridge. Mud packed into molds and dried in the sun made the first bricks. These

About ten thousand years ago, humans began to settle into villages and cities. As cities grew, people needed larger, more permanent buildings. Construction technology became more sophisticated. People began to build monuments, palaces, roads, and bridges. As cities got even bigger, people also needed canals, tunnels, harbors, lighthouses, and sewage systems. Ancient builders learned new techniques and looked for new materials to make new kinds of structures.

ANCIENT ROOTS

You've probably heard people remark, "There's nothing new under the Sun!" That's an exaggeration, of course. Yet there's much truth in the saying when we're talking about construction. Ancient people developed most of our modern building materials, including concrete, glass, bricks, and tiles.

Ancient builders often developed new materials and technology by trial and error. Sometimes they copied and improved on technology used by other cultures. Gradually, ancient builders became more and more skilled. They learned to build bigger, stronger, and more impressive structures.

Many ancient buildings are no longer standing. Some collapsed during earthquakes. Others were destroyed in warfare. Some crumbled after years of neglect. Archaeologists, scientists who study the remains of past cultures, have to piece together clues to guess what these buildings looked like. But in many cases, ancient people wrote about buildings or made pictures of them. So even if a building is gone, modern archaeologists might still know a lot about it.

This book tells the story of ancient building technology—from simple tents and huts to the most awesome palaces and pyramids. Read on to discover the wonders of ancient builders.

CHAPTER ONE

CONSTRUCTION BASICS

The first humans on Earth lived about 2.5 million years ago. They were hunters and gatherers. They lived in small groups and got their food by hunting game, fishing, and gathering wild plants. When the food in one area was all used up, the group moved to a new place. Hunter-gatherers made tools from stone, wood, shells, animal bones, plant fibers, and clay. In some places on Earth, the hunter-gatherer lifestyle remained unchanged until only a few centuries ago. In other places, people gradually gave up hunting and gathering and became herders, farmers, and city dwellers.

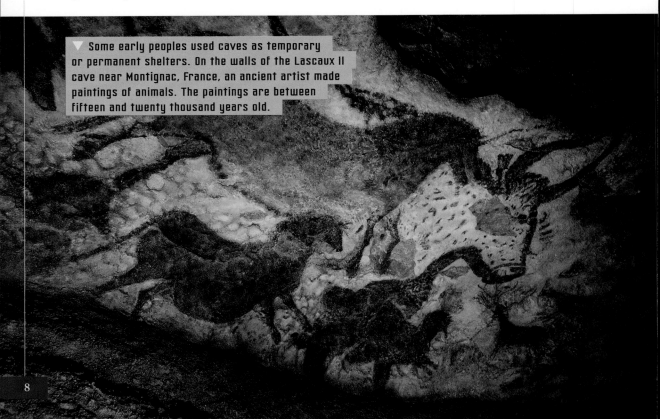

▼ Some early peoples used caves as temporary or permanent shelters. On the walls of the Lascaux II cave near Montignac, France, an ancient artist made paintings of animals. The paintings are between fifteen and twenty thousand years old.

READY-MADE HOMES

Some people think that the earliest humans lived in caves. In fact, we sometimes use the term *cavemen* to refer to early peoples. But very few early peoples were cave dwellers. Caves didn't make pleasant houses. They were damp and dark. Few caves were big enough for a whole family. Even fewer were near reliable supplies of freshwater and game for hunting.

Besides, many caves already had occupants—bears, lions, and hyenas. Imagine trying to move into a cave in ancient times. If you chased the animals out, they might come back in the middle of the night. Bats also make their homes in caves. It would be unpleasant to share a cave with bats that hang upside down from the ceiling and leave droppings all over the floor.

But some early humans, especially in cold places, did live in caves. Because their walls were made of thick layers of earth and stone, caves were often warmer than human-built dwellings. Archaeologists have found evidence of ancient cave dwellings in many places.

One of the oldest cave dwellings ever found is in north central South Africa. Archaeologists have found remains of stone tools showing that people lived in the cave 2 million years ago. Another ancient cave dwelling is near Beijing in southern China. People lived there, generation after generation, between 500,000 and 250,000 years ago.

A cave from ancient Greece contains what might be the first-ever human-made wall. Discovered in 2010, the wall partially blocks the entrance to the Theopetra Cave in central Greece. People probably built the wall to keep cold winds from entering the cave. The structure is twenty-three thousand years old.

BUILD YOUR OWN

Rather than relying on caves, ancient peoples usually built their own homes. They built houses that suited the weather and the landscape that surrounded them. People in warm regions needed buildings with good ventilation, or airflow. People in cold places needed airtight structures that could be heated.

▲ In Mezhyrich, Ukraine, archaeologists unearthed the ruins of an ancient hut made of mammoth bones.

Building materials also depended on the environment. The forests of ancient Europe had plenty of timber, so people there built houses out of wood. Farther to the east, in the Ukraine, ancient peoples made houses of mammoth bones with a covering of animal hides.

GO WITH THE SNOW

Many early peoples made their homes in the Arctic. This is the cold region surrounding the North Pole. One of these groups, the Inuit, made temporary snowhouses called igloos. Igloo builders began by outlining a circle in the snow, about 16 feet (5 meters) across. Then they cut snow blocks out of banks of drifted snow. Each block was about 3 feet (1 m) long, 1.5 feet (0.5 m) high, and 8 inches (20 centimeters) thick. The builders cut each block with a slight curve, to follow the curve of the circle in the snow. They laid a series of blocks in a ring around the base of the circle. They continued to stack blocks to build walls, with each ring of blocks slightly smaller than the one below. This technique created a dome shape, with walls narrowing toward the top of the dome until only a small hole was left. One final block of snow plugged the hole to finish the roof. The builders packed any chinks in the walls with loose snow. They poked one small hole in the top of the dome to let in fresh air.

Once the dome was complete, builders cut an opening at the base of the igloo. They then created a belowground tunnel that served as an entryway. The tunnel trapped cold air and did not allow it to flow inside the house. Builders also hung an animal skin curtain between the tunnel and the igloo's interior.

Inside, igloos were surprisingly warm. People lined the walls with animal hides for insulation (a barrier between warm and cold air). They sat on snow benches lined with moss or sealskin for additional warmth. They lit

BY ANY OTHER NAME

When people hear the term *igloo*, they usually think of snowhouses. But actually the term refers to any Inuit house. Inuit people built igloos of wood, stone, or sod, depending on what materials were available. These houses were permanent structures, designed for long-term housing. Snow igloos, on the other hand, were temporary shelters. Inuit hunters built them quickly and abandoned them when it was time to move to a new hunting area.

This photo from the twentieth century shows an Inuit family building an igloo. Some ancient construction technology remains in use in modern times.

oil lamps for both light and heat. Together, the thick snow walls, animal skin insulation, and oil lamp heating kept cold air out and warm air in. Temperatures inside an igloo could measure 60°F (15.5°C) or even more, even when temperatures outside were below 0°F (-17°C).

PLAYING IT COOL

While ancient peoples in the north developed techniques to make their shelters warm, people in other places wanted to stay cool and dry. Central Africa is hot and rainy year-round. Early peoples there knew how to make light but waterproof huts.

The builders started with thin saplings, or young trees. They stripped each sapling of its bark and bent it to form an arch. They wove a series of sapling arches together to form a dome hut. They used strips of bark or willow branches to tie the saplings together into a solid structure. On top of the skeleton of saplings, builders attached a mat of overlapping leaves. The leaves were large and waxy. They acted like waterproof roofing tiles. Rain hitting the hut ran off the leaves onto the ground, while the people inside stayed dry. Some huts had a large front opening to let in air and light, while others had low, tunnel-like entryways.

MOVING DAY

Hunter-gatherers moved several times a year. In summer they might head to the highlands, where they could gather fruits and nuts and hunt small animals. In winter they might head to the seacoast, where fish were plentiful. Herders too moved often, regularly taking their animals to new pastures. If you had spent time and energy building a sturdy, weatherproof house in one spot, would you want to leave it when it was time to move? Many early peoples did not. Instead, they took apart their shelters piece by piece and carried them to the new location.

For example, on the Great Plains of North America, some Indian peoples lived in tepees. These shelters were fairly easy to build. They were made of a frame of wooden poles, propped together to form a cone. The walls were made of twelve or more buffalo skins sewn together with cord made from animal hide. The skins were draped over the poles. Tent pegs or heavy rocks kept the skins attached to the ground. The tepee door was a place where two skins overlapped to form a flap.

Moving a tepee was pretty easy. Plains Indians pulled out the tent pegs, pulled off the buffalo skin covering, and pulled down the poles. Then they bundled everything up and loaded it onto sleds called travois. Dogs pulled the travois to the new encampment.

▲ Tepees such as this one were easy to build, easy to take down, and easy to move. On the Great Plains of North America, people built tepees through the nineteenth century.

Indians on the Plains probably used this technology for thousands of years. In the 1500s, Spanish explorers came to the Western Hemisphere (North, South, and Central America). They brought the first horses to the Americas. Soon after, Plains Indians began using horses to pull their travois. Since horses could pull bigger loads than dogs could, Plains Indians began making bigger tepees with longer poles. On moving day, horses pulled the long poles on travois.

MONUMENTAL

When we think of construction, we often think of useful structures such as houses and storage sheds. But construction technology includes more than just practical buildings. Ancient peoples often built monuments, such as giant statues. Why were they built? Ancient peoples probably built monuments for the same reason modern people do: to honor their leaders or gods, or to commemorate important events.

One island is famous for its ancient monuments. It is remote Easter Island in the South Pacific Ocean. The island sits 2,300 miles (3,700 kilometers) west of Chile, a nation in South America. Between A.D. 1400 and 1600, Easter Islanders carved nearly nine hundred huge stone statues called *moai*. The statues probably honored the islanders' chiefs or ancestors.

Following a war on the island in 1680, islanders knocked down the moai. Most of them broke. In the late 1900s and early 2000s, archaeologists restored about fifty moai. The archaeologists placed some of the moai in their original positions, looking out over the Pacific Ocean. They placed others in museums. The rest of the moai still lie in pieces around the island.

The statues are figures of people, with giant heads atop torsos. Most are 10 to 20 feet (3 to 6 m) high. A few stand 40 feet (12 m) high. Easter Islanders carved the statues out of soft rock, probably using stone tools.

The moai puzzle archaeologists. The average moai weighs about 14 tons (13 metric tons). One of the largest ever erected weighs 82 tons (74 metric

tons). Islanders carved the statues at rock quarries (deposits) and then moved them to ceremonial sites called *ahus*. In many cases, ahus were several miles from the quarries. Ancient Easter Islanders did not have mechanical equipment such as trucks or cranes. Their only tools were stone, wood, rope, and their own muscles. How did they move the statues?

Several modern archaeologists have attempted to move moai to determine how it was done. One team laid a 10-ton (9-metric-ton) moai on a giant wooden sled, with ropes attached. It took 180 people pulling on the ropes to move the statue. Another research team tried swiveling a moai in the upright position. They attached ropes to the statue's head and base and rocked it from side to side, pivoting the statue forward. Another team used a wooden sled with log rollers underneath. Team members had to constantly reposition the logs to keep the sled moving. Using this method, a team of 25 people moved a 10-ton (9-metric-ton) moai about 150 feet (45 m) in two minutes. But Easter Island has lots of hills and steep terrain. The log-rolling method probably wouldn't have worked over the long haul. After all the studies and experiments, archaeologists still aren't sure how Easter Islanders moved the moai.

ANOTHER MYSTERY: STONEHENGE

One of the biggest mysteries of ancient construction is Stonehenge. This circular stone monument is in Wiltshire County in England, part of Great Britain. Ancient people built the monument between 2800 and 1500 B.C. Archaeologists have to guess at the original appearance of the monument, because over the centuries, some stones have fallen down. People have also carted stones away to build dams, bridges, and other structures.

Archaeologists believe that the original monument was surrounded by a circular ditch and a low wall of piled earth and stone. Inside stood large blocks of gray sandstone arranged in a circle. Each block was about 13 feet (4 m) high and weighed about 28 tons (25 metric tons). Smaller stone slabs rested on top of the big blocks, connecting the whole circle. Within this circle

Blocks of sandstone and bluestone once formed two concentric circles at Stonehenge in England. Other stones were arranged in horseshoe shapes.

was another circle made of sixty smaller bluestones. This inner circle held two additional sets of stones arranged in a horseshoe shape, one inside the other. The horseshoes opened toward the northeast.

> "No one can conceive how such great stones have been so raised aloft, or why they were built here."

—Henry of Huntingdon, English historian, remarking on Stonehenge, A.D. 1130

Who built Stonehenge and why? Some experts think the monument was an ancient religious center. Others think the stones were set up to track astronomical events, such as the summer and winter solstice (the longest and shortest days of the year). The newest theory is that Stonehenge was an ancient graveyard. In 2002 and 2003, archaeologists excavated graves near the site dating to around 2500 B.C. Some of the bodies were buried with gold ornaments, copper knives, pottery, and other finely crafted objects. These objects indicate that the dead were people of wealth and status. Another grave near Stonehenge held the bodies of eight or nine people buried together. These might have been workers who built the monument.

We know little about how Stonehenge was built. People probably dug up earth to create the outer wall using bones, stones, antlers, and their bare hands. But how did they raise the heavy stones into place? Even more mysterious, some of the bluestones came from a mountain range in Wales, 137 miles (220 km) away from Stonehenge. How did ancient people move the stones such a great distance? Archaeologists aren't sure.

THE ANCIENT MIDDLE EAST

Between 10,000 and 3500 B.C., some ancient peoples began abandoning the hunter-gatherer lifestyle. In the ancient Middle East, people began to farm and build permanent villages. One group settled in a region between the Tigris and Euphrates rivers. The region was later named Mesopotamia, which in Greek means "between rivers." In modern times, this area is part of Iraq, Syria, and Turkey.

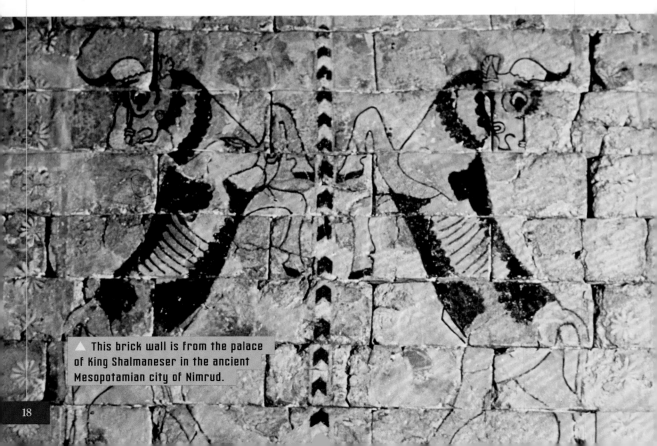

▲ This brick wall is from the palace of King Shalmaneser in the ancient Mesopotamian city of Nimrud.

Mesopotamia was home to a series of ancient peoples, including the Sumerians, Babylonians, and Assyrians. These groups farmed the fertile land along the Tigris and Euphrates rivers. They also built towns and big cities. Some of the world's most important construction technology originated in Mesopotamia.

FROM MUD TO BRICK

Mesopotamia had plenty of clay and mud along the banks of the Tigris and Euphrates rivers. People used these materials to build sturdy and long-lasting houses.

Early on, builders used a construction technique called wattle and daub. The building process began with a simple frame made from long, thin poles or reeds. Builders frequently used a plant called the giant reed, which can grow to be 18 feet (5 m) tall. They wove the reeds or poles together to produce a strong skeleton, called a wattle work. They plastered the wattle work with mud or clay, which hardened in the sun.

Soon the Mesopotamians improved on wattle-and-daub construction. Rather than building whole walls from packed mud and clay, they began to pack clay into small, four-sided wooden frames. The clay dried to create uniform bricks. Builders stacked them to make straight and uniform walls. People in Mesopotamia were making sun-dried bricks as early as 6000 B.C.

Eventually builders realized that mixing chopped straw with mud or clay made bricks stronger. Straw also kept the mud and clay from cracking as bricks dried in the hot sun.

ONE THING LEADS TO ANOTHER

Sometimes a breakthrough in one area of technology provides a breakthrough in another area. For instance, in Mesopotamia brickmakers learned from pottery makers.

The first pottery makers, in the Middle East and other ancient societies, shaped bowls and jugs out of clay and let them dry in the sun. But sun-dried vessels broke easily and sometimes leaked. Then pottery makers discovered that heating pottery in an oven made it much harder, stronger, and more water resistant than sun-dried pottery. In fact, pottery fired in an oven became as hard as stone.

Around 3500 B.C., brickmakers in Mesopotamia began to fire bricks in ovens. Like fired pottery, fired bricks were hard and water resistant.

In ancient Egypt, pottery makers learned to make pottery even stronger. They melted sand and other minerals onto the surface of pottery during firing. This process created a hard glaze, or glasslike coating, on finished pots. Glazed pottery was harder and more waterproof than unglazed pottery. Mesopotamian brickmakers adopted this technology as well. They made glazed bricks with the same kind of waterproof, glasslike coating used on pottery.

BETTER ROOFS

Many ancient houses had thatched roofs. Thatch is a mat of straw, leaves, or branches bundled together. Thatch sheds water well. In ancient times, steeply sloped thatched roofs allowed rainwater to run off houses quickly. People inside the houses stayed dry.

But thatch can't keep out stinging and bloodsucking insects. Thatch also catches on fire easily. In addition, thatch wears out and falls apart.

Homeowners had to replace thatched roofs every few years. This meant taking the whole roof off the house.

Because of thatch's drawbacks, ancient peoples looked for better ways to roof houses. Mesopotamians made a great advance in building technology when they developed clay roofing tiles. Clay tiles, fired like pottery, were longer lasting and more waterproof than thatch. Whereas thatched roofs had to be steeply sloped to shed rainwater, tiled roofs did not. The development of roofing tiles later led to the creation of beautiful buildings, such as classic Greek temples with low-pitched roofs.

A BUILDING MATERIAL FROM HELL

Parts of the Middle East have big underground deposits of petroleum, or crude oil. In modern times, people use petroleum to make many products, including gasoline and asphalt. People in Mesopotamia used petroleum too.

Bitumen is a by-product of petroleum. In some places, bitumen oozes out of the ground, sits in pools, and hardens in the hot sun. At the Dead Sea, a big lake between modern-day Israel and Jordan, bitumen sometimes seeps from the seafloor, hardens, and floats on the surface of the water in huge strands.

The ancient Mesopotamians mixed bitumen (*left*) with straw, sand, and other substances. This mixture made a strong, waterproof mortar to hold bricks in place.

Some Mesopotamians thought that bitumen came from a lake in the "underground," a mythic region believed to be home to evil spirits. But the fear of evil spirits didn't stop ancient Middle Easterners from collecting bitumen. They gathered it from the ground and from the Dead Sea. The modern town of Hit, Iraq, derives its name from bitumen, its main product in ancient times.

Mesopotamians used bitumen as a strong, waterproof mortar between bricks. They also used it as a waterproof coating for walls, sewers, irrigation ditches, and ships. Craftspeople first heated the bitumen to dry up any water it contained. Then they mixed it with substances such as sand, chopped reeds, straw, or powdered limestone. These fillers added thickness, so the mixture didn't run off a wall or other surface to which it was applied. The fillers also made the mortar stronger. Workers processed bitumen right at construction sites and used it immediately while still hot.

ANCIENT SANITATION

Indoor toilets might seem like a modern invention, but the Mesopotamians built indoor toilets thousands of years ago. Mesopotamian toilets were low walls of hardened brick with open seats on top. Toilet floors were coated with bitumen. Inside, toilets opened onto sewer pipes made of rings of fired clay. Sewer pipes were also sealed with bitumen. The pipes carried wastewater to rivers outside of town.

Archaeologists think that only wealthy people in Mesopotamia had indoor toilets. Some Mesopotamian palaces had several toilets lined up side by side. Poor people in Mesopotamia probably used pits dug in the ground as toilets.

BUILDING TO SURVIVE

Ancient town planners designed cities for protection from enemy attacks. City leaders placed important buildings on the tops of hills, because hills were easily defended. Most ancient towns were surrounded by high walls with strong gates.

> "As they dug the fosse [moat], they made bricks of the earth which was carried out of the place they dug, and when they had moulded bricks enough they baked them in ovens; then using hot bitumen for cement and interposing layers of wattled reeds at every thirtieth course of bricks, they build first the border of the fosse and then the wall itself in the same fashion."

—Herodotus, ancient Greek historian, describing construction of the wall around Babylon, fifth century B.C.

The first city walls were simple structures made from heaps of stone and earth. But builders soon learned to make better fortifications out of brick and stone. Babylon was an ancient city-kingdom in Babylonia. Nebuchadrezzar II, who ruled Babylon from 605 to 562 B.C., fortified the city with two sets of brick walls, one inside the other. Each wall was about 23 feet (7 m) thick. The walls were so wide that several chariots could drive side by side along the top. Charioteers and other soldiers could position themselves on top of the walls to fight off attackers. The walls also contained defensive towers that offered extra protection for soldiers. A moat filled with water surrounded the outer wall. Eight gates allowed people to enter and exit the city.

Entrance gates were often the weakest spots in a city wall, so ancient builders took special care to make gates strong and difficult to penetrate. At one Mesopotamian fortress, brick walls lined the road that led to the entrance gate. The road narrowed as it approached the gate. This design forced attackers to crowd tightly together as they rushed toward the gate. Right at the entrance, defenders in high towers could throw rocks, spears, and burning oil onto the crowded attackers.

ONE OF SEVEN WONDERS

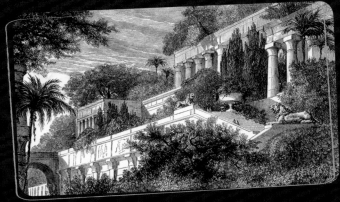

Stories tell of the famous Hanging Gardens of Babylon *(above)*, built by Nebuchadrezzar II in the sixth century B.C. According to the stories, the terraced gardens surrounded the king's hillside palace. Because they were built on terraces, they seemed to hang, suspended in space, from the sides of the palace. They held a fantastic assortment of palm trees, fruiting plants, and flowers. Exotic birds and animals lived among the plants. Sunlight glittered off many waterfalls on the terraces. Apparently, Nebuchadrezzar built the gardens as a gift for his wife, who was homesick for the mountainous countryside of her childhood. We know about the gardens only from descriptions of them written many centuries later.

Archaeologists have never found any actual remnants of the Hanging Gardens. Some experts think the gardens are just a beautiful legend. Whether or not they ever existed, the Hanging Gardens of Babylon are world famous. In the fifth century B.C., a Greek historian named Herodotus listed the Hanging Gardens as one of the Seven Wonders of the Ancient World.

THE ISHTAR GATE

The ancient city of Babylon had eight gates. The most magnificent of these was the Ishtar Gate *(right)*, which led into the city's main street and the king's palace. The original gate had a facade of blue-glazed bricks, decorated with images of lions and dragons. Archaeologists unearthed the remains of the gate in the early twentieth century. They shipped the pieces to a museum in Germany and reconstructed the gate there. Later in the twentieth century, Iraqi president Saddam Hussein built a replica of the gate at its original location near the modern city of Al Hillah. The replica is two-thirds as big as the original.

TOWNS WITH TERRACES

Many Mesopotamian towns included terraces. Terraces are raised mounds of earth or ledges cut into hillsides. Farmers sometimes cut terraces into hillsides to create level ground for planting crops. A terraced hillside resembles the layers on a wedding cake. In some ancient towns, people planted terraces with fruit trees and flowers. Some terraces had buildings on top.

To hold the tons of soil and any buildings that might be erected there, terraces needed strong supporting walls. The walls had to be several feet thick and made from brick or stone. Without supporting walls, the terraces would have collapsed.

It took an amazing amount of work to build terraces. Archaeologists studied one Mesopotamian terrace and concluded that it contained 14 million tons (13 million metric tons) of earth. It probably took twelve thousand workers ten years to move that much soil.

WHAT A TUNNEL!

A tunnel is a horizontal underground passageway. People usually make tunnels by digging through soil or rock. In Babylon an impressive brick-lined tunnel connected the city's royal palace and its temple. The two sites were more than 0.5 miles (0.8 km) apart, on opposite sides of the Euphrates River. The tunnel allowed pedestrians (people on foot) to cross under the river.

Builders started digging the tunnel around 2180 B.C. and finished twenty years later. Archaeologists believe that builders worked during the dry season, when the river was very low. Workers used bitumen to waterproof the brick tunnel.

ZIGGURATS

Mesopotamia was home to many splendid buildings. Some of the most visually dramatic were temple-towers called ziggurats. Ziggurats were built in tiers, or layers. Each tier was a little smaller than the one below. This design made ziggurats look like pyramids with giant steps cut into the sides. People climbed staircases on the outside of a ziggurat to reach a shrine on top. The shrine was a place for worship.

Two ziggurats have become famous. The first is Etemenanki, built in the city of Babylon during the 500s B.C. In modern times, all that remains is the tower's foundation. But when the tower stood in Babylon, it had seven tiers. Its base measured almost 300 feet (91 m) on each side. Its exterior was covered in blue-glazed bricks. Few people probably know the name Etemenanki, but most recognize the name Tower of Babel. This tower is famous from a story in the Bible, a collection of sacred Jewish and Christian

writings from ancient times. The story tells how ancient peoples wanted to build a tower that would reach to heaven. Archaeologists think that Etemenanki inspired the story in the Bible.

Another famous ziggurat is the Ziggurat of Ur. Ur was a walled city in ancient Sumer (in modern-day southeastern Iraq). Built around 2100 B.C., the Ziggurat of Ur was a temple to the Sumerian god Nanna. It was built like many other buildings in Mesopotamia, with mud bricks sealed with bitumen. In modern times, most of the city of Ur lies in ruins. But the base of Ur's ziggurat is still standing. In the twentieth century, people restored parts of the Ziggurat of Ur, including a grand staircase that once took people to the shrine on top.

ANCIENT EGYPT

The Step Pyramid at Saqqara was the first pyramid built in Egypt. Later Egyptian pyramids had sloping sides instead of stepped sides.

Ancient Egypt is famous for its great construction projects. The Egyptians believed that their pharaohs, or kings and queens, were gods. Pharaohs had enormous palaces, monuments, and tombs built in their own honor. Pharaohs wanted to emphasize their great power. They encouraged architects to build massive, awe-inspiring monuments. The most famous monuments from ancient Egypt are giant pyramids.

An Egyptian man named Imhotep was the first engineer and first architect recorded in history. He created the pyramid design that made ancient Egypt so famous. He designed the first pyramid built in Egypt, the Step Pyramid at Saqqara near the Nile River. This limestone monument has six layers, each

one smaller than the layer below. These layers, or steps, give the pyramid its name. The Step Pyramid was built around 2650 B.C. as a tomb for King Djoser.

Archaeologists have found the ruins of more than thirty-five other pyramids along Egypt's Nile River. Three of the most famous were built at Giza, near the modern-day city of Cairo, Egypt. These pyramids were the tombs of pharaohs Khufu, Khafre, and Menkure. The pyramids were made of huge blocks of limestone. Unlike the Step Pyramid, they have sloping sides, with an outer covering of smooth white stones.

THE LARGEST PYRAMID

Khufu's pyramid is the largest Egyptian pyramid. Called the Great Pyramid, it contains more than two million limestone

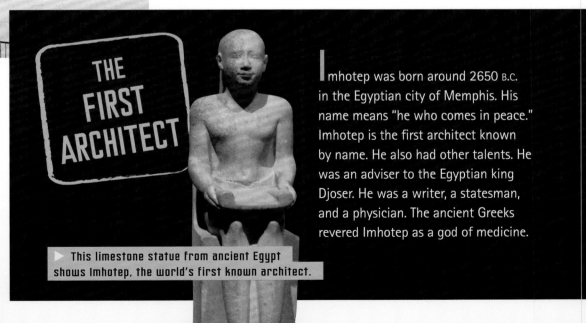

THE FIRST ARCHITECT

Imhotep was born around 2650 B.C. in the Egyptian city of Memphis. His name means "he who comes in peace." Imhotep is the first architect known by name. He also had other talents. He was an adviser to the Egyptian king Djoser. He was a writer, a statesman, and a physician. The ancient Greeks revered Imhotep as a god of medicine.

▶ This limestone statue from ancient Egypt shows Imhotep, the world's first known architect.

▲ The tombs of kings Menkure, Khafre, and Khufu *(from left to right)* are the largest Egyptian pyramids. Egyptian queens are buried in the three smaller pyramids at left.

blocks. They weigh about 3.5 tons (3.2 metric tons) each. That's heavier than two cars. Workers fit the stone blocks together with great precision. The blocks fit so tightly that you can't slip a credit card between them.

The Great Pyramid once rose to a height of 481 feet (146 m). That's as tall as a forty-eight-story skyscraper. Over the centuries, some of the upper stones fell off the pyramid. Thieves also stole the white stones that once formed its smooth outer covering. In modern times, the Great Pyramid stands

"It is a most interesting structure, built of immense masses of rock, fixed together with a great deal of art, and seemingly calculated to last an eternity."

—Ida Pfeiffer, Austrian traveler, on visiting the Great Pyramid in the 1840s about 450 feet (137 m) high. Each side of the base of the pyramid is 755 feet (230 m) long—longer than two football fields. Altogether the pyramid covers an area bigger than ten football fields.

CUTTING PYRAMID STONES

Egyptian stonecutters had a clever way of removing big limestone blocks from stone quarries. They looked for spots where two or three faces of a stone slab were already exposed. They cut narrow grooves into the stone or drilled holes along a line where they wanted to cut. Next, the stonecutters pounded wooden wedges into the holes or grooves. Then they soaked the wedges with water.

Wood swells and expands when it's wet, so the wedges swelled. After about twelve hours, the wedges began to crack the rock along the cut lines.

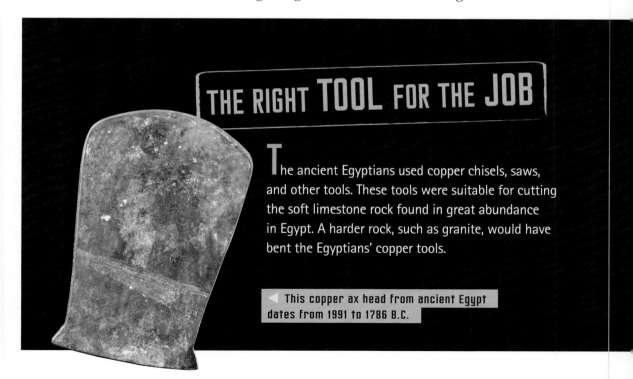

THE RIGHT TOOL FOR THE JOB

The ancient Egyptians used copper chisels, saws, and other tools. These tools were suitable for cutting the soft limestone rock found in great abundance in Egypt. A harder rock, such as granite, would have bent the Egyptians' copper tools.

◄ This copper ax head from ancient Egypt dates from 1991 to 1786 B.C.

As the cracks got bigger, the stonecutters inserted larger wedges. They repeated the steps until the slab of rock broke free. Stonecutters in other ancient civilizations used the same technology.

MOVING PYRAMID STONES

The blocks used to build the pyramids weighed 2 to 5 tons (1.8 to 4.5 metric tons) each. How did workers move such heavy blocks? They first used sledges, or sleds, to pull the blocks from stone quarries to the Nile River. Using rafts, they floated the blocks along the Nile to construction sites.

How did they lift blocks into place on the pyramid itself? As a pyramid rose higher, workers built earthen ramps around its sides. As they added more stones to the pyramid, they made the ramps higher and higher. Using sledges and ropes, laborers hauled the big stones up the ramps. When the pyramid was completed, workers tore down the ramps and hauled the dirt away. Archaeologists have identified remains of earthen ramps at several pyramid sites.

COMPANY TOWNS

Historians believe that the laborers who built the pyramids were ordinary Egyptians. They probably worked on farms most of the year. But during the dry season, when there was little farmwork to do, they built pyramids and other monuments for the pharaohs. Each building project involved about ten thousand workers.

Archaeologists digging at Giza have found traces of the workers who made the pyramids. They have found mud brick tombs holding the bodies of ordinary workers and their families. Larger limestone tombs hold the bodies of supervisors. Archaeologists have studied the skeletons of the ordinary workers. Their spines show signs of great stress, indicating that the workers carried heavy loads and did hard physical labor.

Along with the graves, archaeologists have found the remains of settlements where the pyramid builders lived. They have found the ruins of

mud brick houses, stone walls, streets, workshops, bakeries, kitchens, storage buildings, and sleeping barracks. They have also found pottery vessels, stones for grinding grain, and other household tools once used by the vast army of workers at Giza.

WATERWORKS

In addition to pyramids, temples, and other monuments, the Egyptians built many practical structures. They built canals for shipping and canals for irrigation, or carrying water to crops. They built dams to store water for drinking and farming. They also built sewers and toilets.

What may be the oldest dam in the world was built in Egypt in about 2900 B.C. It was located on a river southwest of Cairo. The dam was about 350 feet (107 m) long, 37 feet (11 m) high, and 78 feet (24 m) thick in some places. It was made of limestone blocks. Ancient Egyptians built the dam to store water for workers in nearby stone quarries.

Like the Mesopotamians, the Egyptians built toilets and drains. Some Egyptian toilets were quite elaborate, with copper drainpipes for carrying away waste material. Other toilets were simple stone boxes that had to be emptied by hand. People probably placed clay pots in the bottoms of these toilets to make removing waste easier. Egyptian toilet seats were made of wood or stone.

ANCIENT INDIA

People in western India began settling into villages around 4000 B.C. They built the same kind of wattle-and-daub huts found in early Mesopotamia. Within one thousand years, one of the world's greatest civilizations had emerged in this region. It covered an area of around 300,000 square miles (777,000 sq. km) in modern-day Pakistan and India. Known as the Indus Valley Civilization, it developed along the Indus River.

The Indus Valley Civilization lasted for one thousand years, from about 3000 to 2000 B.C. Then the people abandoned their towns and cities. Experts think that over time, the rivers that Indus Valley people used for water and transportation might have changed course. These changes created floods in some places and left other places without enough water. So people abandoned their cities for better-watered lands to the east.

LOST AND FOUND

After the Indus Valley Civilization ended, its cities and buildings fell into ruin. In some places, new cities sprang up over the ruins. As the centuries passed, the Indus Valley Civilization was forgotten, although local people knew about some of the ruins. A few foreign travelers visited some of the ruins in the 1800s. In 1921 archaeologists began excavating two Indus Valley sites, Mohenjo Daro and Harappa. Eventually archaeologists uncovered the remains of hundreds of other settlements in the region.

Archaeologists believe that Mohenjo Daro had a population of about forty thousand. Harappa might have been home to thirty-five thousand people. Archaeologists have also excavated other Indus Valley towns. Several of them were probably as large as Mohenjo Daro.

At Mohenjo Daro, archaeologists have found the ruins of a large bathhouse. Several sets of stairs led down into the water, where people purified themselves during religious ceremonies.

"When I joined the camp I found it in front of the village and ruinous brick castle. Behind us was a large circular mound . . . and to the west was an irregular rocky height, crowned with the remains of buildings, in fragments of walls, with niches, after the eastern manner."

—Charles Masson, British soldier who saw the ruins of Harappa in the late 1820s

TOWN PLANNING

Harappa and Mohenjo Daro are among the earliest examples of planned towns. Planners used the same approach for both cities. A huge brick and timber building stood in the center of town. Built on a platform of packed earth and stone and surrounded by high walls, the building served as a protective fortress and government center. The fortress at Mohenjo Daro held a large bathhouse. People probably used it for religious ceremonies.

City streets spread out from the fortress in a grid pattern. Major streets ran north and south, east and west. The main streets ranged from 9 to 34 feet (3 to 10 m) wide. Homes, shops, and other buildings lined the streets.

Homes had solid front walls, with no windows or doors facing the street. This arrangement gave residents privacy and also helped protect houses from thieves. Doors were located in the backs of the houses. People reached them by narrow paths behind the main streets. The doors often opened into courtyards, where people probably ate and worked in good weather.

Most Indus Valley homes had two stories, high ceilings, and flat roofs. They were built according to the same plan. Brick staircases inside the houses

▲ This chesslike board game from an Indus Valley city shows that ancient Indian games and pastimes were not all that different from our own.

led to upper floors and rooftops. Walls were made from big, flat bricks, about 10 inches (25 cm) wide, 20 inches (50 cm) long, and 3.5 inches (9 cm) thick. The thick brick walls and high ceilings helped keep houses cool in summer.

A TON OF BRICKS

Ancient Indian brickmakers stacked clay bricks into mounds that resembled beehives. The brickmakers lit fires underneath the mounds and kept them burning for hours, until the bricks were hardened like pottery. This method allowed brickmakers to harden large numbers of bricks all at once.

Ancient Indus Valley bricks were used a second time in the 1850s, thousands of years after they were made. At that time, Britain controlled much of India. British railroad engineers gathered bricks from Harappa and used them on railroad construction projects.

ANCIENT PLUMBING

Mohenjo Daro and Harappa had some of the ancient world's most advanced toilets and drains. The city streets were lined with brick sewers. People got drinking and bathing water from underground brick-lined wells. Usually, one well served an entire neighborhood.

Some houses had bathrooms and toilets. People probably flushed the toilet with a pitcher of water after each use. Wastes traveled down a drainpipe to underground sewers that drained into a nearby river. This system probably allowed disease to spread, because people living downstream from the town used the same river for drinking and bathing.

The bathhouse at Mohenjo Daro was a large brick building with dressing rooms and a central courtyard. The courtyard contained a bathing pool. It was about 40 feet (12 m) long, 23 feet (7 m) wide, and 8 feet (2.4 m) deep. Two flights of stairs led into the water. The pool was built from clay bricks. Builders added layers of bitumen to make the pool waterproof. Scholars think that people in Mohenjo Daro used the bath for religious reasons. They went into the water to purify themselves during religious ceremonies.

▼ Ancient Indus Valley people built this brick-lined well to store drinking water. Many families probably shared the well.

THE WORLD'S FIRST DOCK?

The Indus Valley city of Lothal was much like Harappa and Mohenjo Daro. It was a planned town, with brick buildings, bathrooms, and sewers. Lothal sat on the banks of the Sabarmati River. The river emptied into the Gulf of Khambhat, an arm of the Arabian Sea.

People from other Indus Valley towns shipped goods by riverboat to Lothal. From there, boats traveled into the Arabian Sea. They carried goods west to Mesopotamia, Arabia, and Egypt. In turn, traders from the west sailed to Lothal with cargo. Riverboats then carried the cargo upriver to other Indus Valley cities. The ships carried trade goods such as barley, wheat, cotton, ivory, gold, and timber.

Archaeologists think that Lothal might have contained the world's oldest known dockyards. They have found the remains of a brick structure measuring 122 feet (37 m) by 73 feet (22 m). Built around 2400 B.C., the structure sat alongside the Sabarmati River. In modern times, however, the river takes a different course.

Boats coming downriver or from the Gulf of Khambhat might have sailed into the structure at high tide. Once the boats were inside, a watertight gate kept the water from rushing back into the river. The gate kept water at the same level, whether the tide was low or high. That way, ships were always level with the dock. This technology allowed ancient Indus Valley workers to load and unload ships twenty-four hours a day. A long wharf connected the dockyard to a warehouse.

Some archaeologists question this theory, however. They think the structure at Lothal might have simply been a large tank for storing water.

ANCIENT CHINA

▲ Not only did ancient Chinese people live in cave houses, some modern Chinese people do as well. This site in northern China holds cave houses carved into cliffs.

People in ancient China lived in different kinds of houses, depending on the climate and nearby resources. In many places, ancient Chinese people built wattle-and-daub houses. In wet regions, people built houses on stilts, so their floors remained dry when the ground below was wet. In forested regions, they built houses of wood.

Some Chinese people created cave dwellings by digging into loess. Loess is a yellowish soil made of fine mineral particles. In some places, loess covers the ground. Other places have cliffs made of loess. In parts of northern and northwestern China, people carved out houses by digging into loess cliffs.

▼ This modern illustration shows Chinese workers pounding soil to build an earthen wall.

They sometimes plastered the interior walls of their cave houses with mud and strengthened the roofs with wooden supports.

Rammed earth was another common building material in ancient China. Builders first made a hollow wooden frame in the shape of a low wall. Then they dumped loose wet soil into the frame. They mixed in straw and other substances to strengthen the soil. Builders then pounded down the mixture with heavy poles. The pounding compressed the soil, making it very dense. As the soil dried, it hardened. When builders removed the wooden frame, they were left with a hard earthen wall. They could repeat the process to build the house foundation or sometimes all the walls. Ancient Chinese people used this same method to build defensive walls around their cities and towns.

KEEPING WARM

In the northern half of the world, strong cold winds blow from the north. For this reason, people in ancient China often made the northern walls of their houses thicker than the other walls. The extra thickness helped keep houses warm. Chinese people built doors to their houses in the south-facing walls. South-facing doorways let in sunlight but not cold northern winds.

Many ancient Chinese people created pit houses. They dug a shallow pit in the ground. The bottom of the pit became the house's floor. The sides of the pit formed the bottoms of walls. Then people extended the walls upward using wood, mud, or reeds. Pit houses stayed warmer than houses built entirely above the ground, because the earthen walls and floors were good insulation.

To keep people even warmer, Chinese inventors created one of the world's first central heating systems. The system was simple but effective. Builders made houses with raised stone floors, with an empty space between the floor and the ground. Homeowners lit a fire in the space beneath the floor. The heat traveled across the stone to warm the entire house.

▼ Inside the Banpo Museum in Xi'an, China, staff have built an ancient-style mud-and-timber house. People in this part of China lived in similar houses more than six thousand years ago.

MASTER BUILDERS

The ancient Chinese were skilled carpenters. They learned to fit pieces of timber together to make strong, interlocking joints. They used the mortise and tenon design. In this system, a projecting piece of wood (a tenon) from one beam fits tightly into a hole, a groove, or a slot (a mortise) of another beam. Archaeologists have found evidence of mortise and tenon construction from the ruins of the ancient Hemudu culture in southeastern China. The ruins date to 5000 B.C.

At first Chinese people covered their homes with thatched roofs. But like builders in Mesopotamia, they eventually learned to make clay roofing tiles. By A.D. 100, the Chinese had started to build with brick. Later, Chinese architects adorned buildings with glazed tiles and carved stones.

THE GREAT WALL OF CHINA

The Great Wall of China was the largest construction project of the ancient world. Counting all the curves and bends, the wall stretches for more than 4,500 miles (7,240 km) across northern China. Ancient Chinese leaders built the wall to protect China from northern invaders.

The Great Wall was not the first border wall in China. Other protective walls date to the 600s B.C. In the 200s B.C., Emperor Qin Shi Huangdi decided to build the Great Wall as protection against invaders.

Watchtowers spaced at regular intervals along the Great Wall allowed soldiers to guard against invaders.

Builders used whatever materials were available nearby to make the wall. They used stone in some parts and rammed earth in others. They always covered the outside and top of the wall with a layer of stone or brick. Construction continued on and off for hundreds of years.

Workers did not build the whole wall from scratch. They connected brand-new sections with walls that were already standing. The wall wound over mountains and through valleys. But it never formed a continuous barrier across northern China. In some places, sections were not connected.

The Great Wall averages about 30 feet (9 m) in height. Its base is about

Since the Great Wall runs across mountains, builders included stairways to help people walk up and down.

NOT SO GREAT

Workers built the Great Wall across the rugged terrain of northern China.

The Great Wall of China was an effective defense against small-scale attacks, but it could not keep out Genghis Khan's army. The great leader of the Mongol people invaded China between 1211 and 1223 A.D. As his army entered China, it traveled through areas where the Great Wall had crumbled or had never been connected in the first place. The Mongols ruled China until 1368.

25 feet (7.6 m) thick, narrowing to about 15 feet (4.6 m) at the top. A paved road runs along the top of the wall. Originally the road allowed workers and soldiers to travel along the wall. The wall contains about twenty thousand watchtowers, which helped soldiers keep a lookout for enemies. The towers are spaced about 250 feet (76 m) apart. Deep ditches on the northern side of the wall provided an extra line of defense against invaders.

Most of the original wall collapsed over the centuries. In the late 1400s, China's government rebuilt some of the wall. The government restored parts of the wall again in the 1980s. In modern times, the wall is a famous tourist attraction. More than 40 million foreign tourists visit the wall each year.

THE ANCIENT AMERICAS

North, South, and Central America were once home to great ancient civilizations. Few written records remain from these groups, but excavations reveal that ancient American technology was very advanced. Throughout the Americas, ancient peoples built impressive houses, buildings, and monuments.

MYSTERIOUS HEADS

The Olmec civilization flourished in Mexico between 1200 and 400 B.C. Among the artifacts (human-made objects) left by the Olmecs are giant, carved stone heads. Archaeologists have found seventeen heads, most of them at a site called San Lorenzo in southern Mexico. The heads stand 4.5 to 9 feet (1.4 to 2.7 m) tall. They weigh 8 to 12 tons (7.25 to 10.9 metric tons) each.

OLDER THAN THE OLMEC

▲ At Caral, Peru, archaeologists have found the remains of stepped stone pyramids.

For many years, archaeologists thought the Olmec were the first people in the Americas to live in cities. But in 2001, archaeologists announced that Caral, a settlement in Peru, was much older than any Olmec city. They determined that Caral was founded before 2600 B.C., more than one thousand years before the Olmec. Caral was once home to about

This giant head is one of many Olmec carvings inside La Venta Park in Villahermosa, Mexico.

three thousand people. Archaeologists have found the remains of government offices, public plazas, workshops, and houses, indicating that it was once a thriving city. The most prominent buildings in the town were six stepped stone pyramids with staircases leading to the top.

To find out how old Caral was, archaeologists used a technique called radiocarbon dating. All living things contain a substance called radiocarbon. After something dies, its radiocarbon turns into nitrogen. This conversion happens at a uniform rate. By comparing the amount of radiocarbon in a dead organism to the amount of nitrogen, archaeologists can apply a formula and tell how long the organism has been dead. Archaeologists arrived at the 2600 B.C. date by measuring the amount of radiocarbon and nitrogen in bags woven from plant fibers discovered at Caral.

They have flat faces, thick lips, and helmetlike hats resembling those worn by modern football players. Scholars think that the heads were created to honor Olmec rulers.

The heads were carved from a volcanic rock called basalt. The rock came from mountains more than 40 miles (64 km) from where the heads stand. Archaeologists don't know how the Olmecs moved such heavy blocks of stone that far. It probably took hundreds of laborers many months to move the stones into place.

MAYAN PYRAMIDS

After the Olmecs, other civilizations emerged in Mexico and Central America. Mayan culture flourished between A.D. 250 and 900. The Maya built large cities with magnificent stone temple-pyramids, palaces, and other buildings. One city, Tikal (in modern-day Guatemala), had a population of fifty thousand.

The ancient Maya gathered at the Kukulkan Pyramid in southeastern Mexico for religious ceremonies. Kukulkan was a Mayan snake god.

The Mayan city of Chichén Itzá (in southeastern Mexico) was built in the fifth or sixth century A.D. The city is famous for its huge temple-pyramids. Historians think the Maya conducted bloody ceremonies at the pyramids. With thousands of people gathered around, guards forced prisoners of war to climb stairs to the top of a pyramid. When each prisoner reached the top, a holy man sliced open his chest with a razor-sharp stone knife and pulled out his still-beating heart. Blood flowed down the stairs, toward the captives who were still climbing.

At the city's Kukulkan Pyramid, hand-clapping below the stairways produces strange, high-pitched echoes. Some scientists believe that the sounds are no accident. Ancient Mayan builders may have designed the stairways as acoustic chambers. They were able to amplify and change sounds. Some scientists think the builders were trying to reproduce the song of the quetzal, a bird that was sacred to the Maya.

Other Mayan cities also had impressive temple-pyramids. Pyramids at Tikal stand more than 200 feet (60 m) tall. Pyramids at Palenque in southeastern Mexico are covered with intricately carved hieroglyphics, or picture writing. Pyramids at Tulum, on Mexico's Yucatán Peninsula, might have been used as astronomical observatories. Scientists

The Maya used picture-writing to record information about astronomy, religion, and daily life. This writing was carved on a temple in Palenque, a Mayan city in Mexico.

have noted how the small windows of the temples line up with certain movements of the sun, the stars, and the planets.

WATER YEAR-ROUND

La Milpa was a Mayan city in modern-day Belize in Central America. Like many other Mayan cities, La Milpa had a huge public square paved with cobblestones. This 4-acre (1.6-hectare) square, or Great Plaza, probably served as a marketplace and gathering spot. But archaeologists believe that the square was also a key part of the Maya's water supply system.

The region surrounding La Milpa had few rivers or other permanent sources of water. Water would have been very scarce during the long dry season, from November to May. How did the Maya get water for their crops and to drink?

Archaeologists think the Maya caught and stored water that fell during the rainy season. At La Milpa, water ran off the cobblestones of the Great Plaza into a series of drainage canals, dams, and reservoirs. These structures were very simple, built from stone blocks and packed clay. They were very effective for gathering and storing water.

CLEVER DESIGNERS

Mayan houses had walls of flat stones layered one on top of another. To make roofs for the houses, Mayan builders developed a clever design called a corbeled roof. When house walls had been completed to their final height, builders laid another row of stones over the inner edges of the walls. This row reached just slightly into the interior of the building. Then the builders placed another layer of stones and another, each reaching into the interior a bit more. Eventually, the layers met in the center of the house to complete the roof. Builders had to take great care, though. The roof could not be too wide, or it would collapse under its own weight. Built right, corbeled roofs were very strong and lasted for centuries.

ANCIENT SAUNAS

People in many ancient cultures built saunas, or sweathouses. Saunas helped ancient peoples stay clean and healthy and keep warm. Sick people probably used saunas for relief from fevers, arthritis, and other ailments. Sometimes ancient peoples used saunas for religious ceremonies as well.

The ancient Maya were master sauna builders. Their sweathouses, called *temazcalli*, were built from stone. Heat came from a fire pit in the sauna floor or wall. People sat or squatted inside the sauna. They threw water onto glowing coals or hot stones to create steam.

CLIFF DWELLERS

The Ancestral Puebloans, sometimes called Anasazi, lived in North America from the first century A.D. to about 1300. They occupied the Four Corners region of the United States, the meeting place of the modern-day states of

People once lived beneath the cliffs of Mesa Verde in Colorado. In the twenty-first century, the cliff dwellings are part of a national park.

Colorado, New Mexico, Utah, and Arizona. Some Ancestral Puebloans lived in pit houses, with earthen walls and thatched roofs. Others built houses from adobe, or sun-dried bricks.

In southern Colorado, in a place called Mesa Verde (a modern-day national park), the Ancestral Puebloans built fabulous houses and other structures high above the ground, beneath overhanging cliffs. Created in the 1200s, the buildings look like giant apartment complexes. The towering cliff walls helped protect residents from the weather, wild animals, and enemies. People had to climb up steep trails and rock-cut stairways to reach their houses.

To make their cliff dwellings, the Ancestral Puebloans shaped local sandstone into building blocks. They stacked the blocks in layers to make walls. They made mortar from a mixture of soil, water, and ashes. Along with mortar, they also pressed tiny pieces of hard stone between the sandstone blocks. The hard stone helped strengthen the walls of the dwellings. Builders added a final layer of mud plaster. The plaster was pink, brown, red, yellow, or white, depending on the color of the minerals in mud.

Visitors to Mesa Verde often wonder about the low doorways leading into dwellings and other structures. Modern people have to bend over to enter. But in Ancestral Puebloan times, the doorways were a better fit. The average Ancestral Puebloan man was only about 5 feet 4 inches (163 cm) tall. The average woman was about 5 feet (152 cm).

INCA BUILDERS

In the 1400s and 1500s, the Inca Empire ruled a vast territory in South America. The empire included parts of present-day Colombia, Ecuador, Peru, Chile, Bolivia, and Argentina. The Inca were skilled builders. When making a wall or building, they cut the stones very precisely. The precision cutting allowed each stone to fit tightly against the ones next to it. By fitting the stones this way, the Inca could make structures without using mortar.

"Here there was an extensive level space, with very sumptuous and majestic buildings, erected with great skill and art, all the lintels of [beams above] the doors, the principal as well as the ordinary ones, being of marble, elaborately carved."

—Spanish soldier Baltasar de Ocampo, describing an Inca city, late 1500s

The most famous Inca archaeological site is Machu Picchu. This city in the Andes Mountains of Peru is filled with the remains of temples, palaces, stairways, storehouses, burial grounds, irrigation channels, and agricultural terraces. All the buildings were carefully crafted from stone. Archaeologists think the city was a royal estate for Inca rulers.

A vast network of roads and bridges connected different parts of Inca territory. In some places, the bridges spanned vast river gorges. Inca builders used simple technology to make bridges that were both long and strong. First, they wove long ropes out of plant fibers. Then they braided many ropes together to make thick cables. The length of the cables depended on the distance to be spanned. In some cases, cables were 150 feet (46 m) long or longer. Five cables formed the framework of the bridge. Two of these cables were handrails. Three other cables served as the bridge floor. Bridge builders attached the five cables to stone supports on both sides of the gorge.

OLD TECHNOLOGY, NEW BRIDGE

One Inca rope bridge is still in use. In the town of Huinchiri, Peru, people gather each year to maintain an old Inca bridge over the Apurimac River *(right)*. They hold a three-day festival to gather stiff grasses and braid them into cables. They replace worn-out cables from the previous year to keep the bridge strong.

Builders wove shorter cables to connect the handrails and the floor of the bridge. They attached pieces of wood to the floor cables to create a solid surface for walking. They attached more wood and branches along the side cables to create walls. Inca bridges swayed in the fierce winds that sometimes blew through river gorges, but they were strong enough to hold both people and animals. To keep the bridges safe and strong, local people replaced most of the fiber cables each year.

ANCIENT GREECE

Twenty-five hundred years ago, the Acropolis was the most important spot in Athens. It was the center of government, art, and religious worship.

Pericles was a leader of Athens, a city in ancient Greece. In a famous speech in 431 B.C., he said, "Mighty indeed are the marks and monuments in our empire which we have left. Future ages will wonder at us, as the present wonders at us now."[7] Pericles was correct. Modern people still marvel at ancient Greek buildings and copy their designs.

Pericles lived from about 495 to 429 B.C. His home, Athens, was a great center of learning, art, and culture. One of the city's most famous sites was its acropolis. An acropolis is a group of temples, theaters, and government buildings on a hill overlooking a city. Many Greek cities had acropolises. But the acropolis in Athens was the most spectacular. It eventually became known throughout the world as *the* Acropolis.

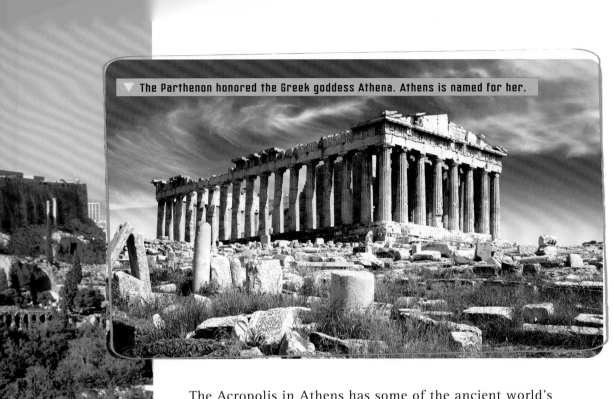

▼ The Parthenon honored the Greek goddess Athena. Athens is named for her.

The Acropolis in Athens has some of the ancient world's most famous architecture. One building is the Parthenon, built between 447 and 432 B.C. This temple honored Athena, the Greek goddess of warfare, wisdom, and arts and crafts. Athena was also the patron goddess, or protector, of Athens. The elegant Parthenon was framed by columns on the outside. More columns lined its two interior chambers. A magnificent gold and ivory statue of Athena stood inside the temple. Light entered the inner chambers through bronze gates. In modern times, the temple stands in ruins, but many of its columns and architectural features are still intact.

Another building at the Acropolis, the Erechtheum, honored Athena, Poseidon (the Greek god of the sea), and the legendary Greek king Erechtheus. The Propylaea was a beautiful marble entranceway into the Acropolis itself.

TRICKING THE EYE

Seen from a distance, the Parthenon's marble columns and other architectural elements appear straight and perfectly proportioned. Actually, some of these elements were made deliberately out of proportion. Greek architects knew that perfectly even buildings, when viewed from certain angles, create an optical illusion. They appear crooked and uneven.

For this reason, Greek architects made the Parthenon's end columns a little thicker than its central columns. That way, they all appeared equal from a distance. Architects spaced the end columns closer together than the central columns for the same reason. All the columns bulge a little at the center, but they look perfectly straight from a distance. In addition, the Parthenon's steps curve upward slightly, but they appear flat from a distance.

▲ The Erechtheum at the Acropolis in Athens had Ionic columns like this one.

GREEK COLUMNS

No part of ancient Greek architecture is more classically "Greek" than the long rows of marble columns in temples. Built in the 500s B.C., the Temple of Artemis at the city of Ephesus (in modern-day Turkey) was one of the Seven Wonders of the Ancient World. It is remembered for its 106 columns, lined up in perfect rows. Each column was about 67 feet (20 m) tall.

Greek builders used three basic types of columns: Doric, Ionic, and Corinthian. Each style has a long central shaft, lined with narrow grooves called flutes. The bases and

Ancient Greek builders used series of stone columns to hold up stone roofs. These columns supported the Temple of Poseidon near Athens.

capitals (tops) of columns have different kinds of carvings, depending on the style.

When building temples, Greek architects often followed formulas. These rules told architects what kinds of columns and how many to use, how big the columns should be, and how much space to leave between them. One popular temple style featured a frame of columns around the building and six columns out front. Even with the formulas, Greek architects could use their own creativity in designing the details of temples and other buildings.

Greek builders used lots of columns for good reason. They mostly built with stone. Roofs and doorways were made of stone slabs laid across the tops of stone columns. Without enough support, stone can be very weak. In fact, a long stone slab will break under its own weight unless supported by a lot of columns. So the Greeks had to build structures with lots of columns or their roofs and doorways would have fallen down.

As structures became more complex in ancient Greece, building became more of a science. Builders also had to be mathematicians and engineers.

They had to calculate exactly how much weight a slab of stone could hold before cracking. They had to space columns correctly. If columns were placed too far apart, the stone slabs bridging the gaps between them would crack. Builders didn't want to space columns too close together either. Columns were very expensive to carve and assemble, so using too many columns was a waste of money.

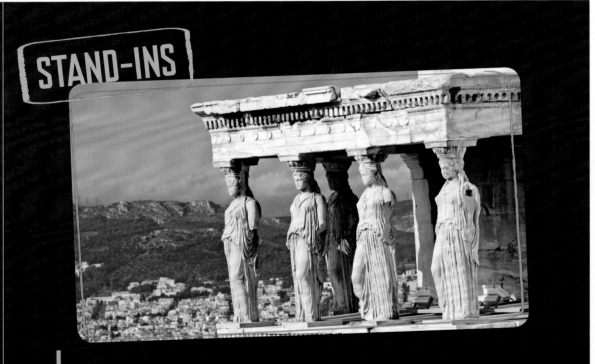

STAND-INS

In some Greek buildings, such as the Erechtheum, columns were carved in the shape of human figures. Columns in the shape of females are called caryatids *(above)* and were named for Greek priestesses. Those in the shape of males are called atlantes and were named for Atlas. Atlas was a character from Greek myth who held up the sky on his shoulders.

A BEAUTIFUL TOWN

One of the most famous cities in the ancient world was Alexandria, Egypt. A general named Alexander founded the city after conquering Egypt in 331 B.C. Alexander was born in Macedonia, north of Greece, and was schooled by the Greek philosopher Aristotle. Alexander grew to revere Greek culture. Alexandria became a cultural and educational center for the Greek-speaking world.

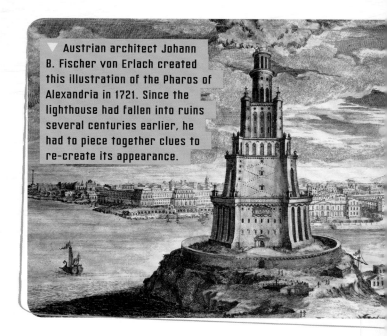

▼ Austrian architect Johann B. Fischer von Erlach created this illustration of the Pharos of Alexandria in 1721. Since the lighthouse had fallen into ruins several centuries earlier, he had to piece together clues to re-create its appearance.

Alexander hired Dinocrates, a Greek architect, to create a plan for Alexandria. The city had seven wide streets running parallel to the coast of the Mediterranean Sea. Eleven other streets intersected these seven at right angles. The longest street, the Canopic Way, was about 3.5 miles (5.6 km) long.

The lighthouse at Alexandria was another wonder of the ancient world. It was called the Pharos because it was built on the island of Pharos, just off the city's coast. Construction lasted from 283 to 246 B.C. The lighthouse consisted of three huge marble towers, built one on top of the other. Its total height was 384 feet (117 m). A statue of Zeus, king of the Greek gods, sat on top of the lighthouse. Inside the upper tower, workers tended a fire that guided ships safely into Alexandria's harbor at night. A polished bronze reflector made the light from the fire even brighter. Sailors could see the light from 30 miles (48 km) away. The Pharos operated for about fifteen hundred years. Strong earthquakes in the 1300s damaged the Pharos, and it fell into ruins.

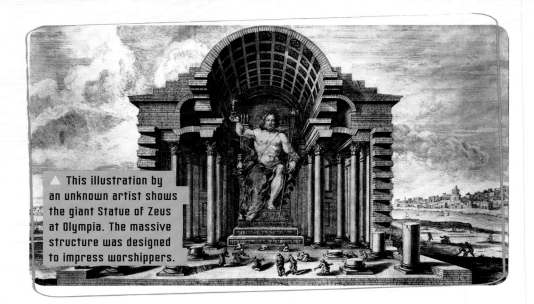

This illustration by an unknown artist shows the giant Statue of Zeus at Olympia. The massive structure was designed to impress worshippers.

STATUESQUE

Many ancient cultures built giant statues to honor people and gods. The ancient Greeks were no exception. Two ancient Greek statues were on the Seven Wonders list. They were the Statue of Zeus (the king of Greek gods) at Olympia (in Greece) and the Colossus of Rhodes. (Rhodes is a Greek island.)

The people of Olympia had a temple to honor Zeus. But they also wanted a statue of Zeus inside the temple. About 430 B.C., they hired a sculptor named Phidias to create the statue. Phidias's statue was 43 feet (13 m) tall. It had an inner framework of wood, covered by sheets of metal and ivory. The figure of Zeus was seated on a throne that was inlaid with precious stones. The design was clever. Zeus looked as if he were about to stand up and smash through the roof of the temple. People traveled great distances to worship at the temple. Viewing platforms even enabled visitors to climb up and inspect Zeus's face. In the second century A.D., the Greek writer Pausanias described the statue:

> On his head lies a sculpted wreath of olive sprays. On his right hand he holds a figure of Victory made from ivory and gold. . . . In his left hand the god holds his sceptre [staff] inlaid with every kind of metal, and the bird perched on the sceptre

—Roman writer Pliny the Elder, describing the toppled Colossus of Rhodes, first century A.D.

is an eagle. The sandals of the god are made of gold, as is his robe . . . . The throne is decorated with gold and precious stones, with ebony and ivory.

The other statue on the Seven Wonders list, the Colossus of Rhodes, stood in the Greek port city of Rhodes, on the island of the same name. It was a giant statue of Helios, the Greek god of the Sun. A Greek sculptor named Chares of Lindos designed the statue. Construction began in 294 B.C. and continued for twelve years. The statue had an iron framework covered with sheets of bronze. Workers built from the ground up, filling the statue's legs with stones to keep it from tipping over. By building a spiral earthen ramp around the statue as they worked, laborers were able to reach the figure's upper portions. The completed statue was 110 feet (33 m) high—taller than a ten-story building. It stood for about fifty years, until an earthquake in 226 B.C. knocked most of it down. Only the knees and lower legs were left standing. In A.D. 654, Syrian soldiers conquered Rhodes. They took the remaining bronze covering of the statue back to Syria. The Syrians probably melted the bronze to make coins.

▲ The Colossus of Rhodes stood taller than a ten-story building.

ANCIENT ROME

The Pantheon in Rome, Italy, features two ancient Roman contributions to construction: concrete and a domed roof.

Ancient Rome began as a small city around 900 B.C. Over the following centuries, the ancient Romans built a great empire. It began in their home base of Italy. By the first century A.D., it reached all the way to central Europe, the Middle East, and northern Africa. Throughout their empire, the Romans constructed impressive bridges, roads, and buildings. They made bigger and stronger structures than any other ancient builders. How did they do it?

The Romans made great buildings by borrowing construction technology from neighboring peoples and then improving on it. From the Greeks, the

Romans borrowed the idea of magnificent public buildings. From the Etruscans, who preceded the Romans in Italy, the Romans borrowed the arch. The Romans also developed an important construction technology of their own—concrete. With concrete the Romans could build huge domes, long bridges, and giant stadiums.

The ancient Romans approached architecture as both an art and a science. Many Roman architects learned their craft from a book called *De Architectura* (On Architecture). Marcus Vitruvius, a Roman architect and engineer, wrote the book around 27 B.C. *De Architectura* dealt with all aspects of construction, including building materials, flooring, construction of temples and other public buildings, and even the education of architects. Vitruvius wrote that an architect "should be a man of letters, a skilled draughtsman, a mathematician, familiar with scientific thought, a diligent student of philosophy, acquainted with music, not ignorant of medicine."

ARCS OF TRIUMPH

Several Roman emperors created triumphal arches in their own honor. These arches were more decorative than practical. They were carved with words and images honoring the emperor's deeds. The Arch of Constantine *(above)* was just one of many triumphal arches in the city of Rome. Still standing in modern times, it measures 69 feet (21 m) high, 84 feet (26 m) wide, and 24 feet (7 m) deep. It commemorates Emperor Constantine's victory over his rival Maxentius at the Battle of Milvian Bridge in A.D. 312.

RAISING THE ROOF

An arch is a curved structure that spans an opening, such as a window or a doorway. Arches are strong. Unlike the flat stone slabs above doorways and walls in ancient Greek temples, arches don't collapse under their own weight. The Romans were the first ancient people to make widespread use of arches in building. With arches, Roman builders could cover open spaces without using long rows of stone columns underneath.

The simplest arches span doorways and windows. A series of arches set against one another can be used to cover a rectangular space. This kind of ceiling is called a vault. Domes are also based on the arch design. A domed roof or ceiling looks like a basketball cut in half. The dome covers a circular or square space.

The Roman-era Alcantara Bridge crosses the Tagus River in Spain. Modern travelers can cross the river on a new bridge nearby.

BUILDING BETTER BRIDGES

The Romans realized that arches were perfect for building strong bridges. The idea was simple. The arch's two legs rested on a riverbank. The curved, upper part of the arch supported the roadway over the river. The two legs on the riverbanks carried the weight of the arch, the road, and the travelers on the bridge.

The Romans built arched bridges throughout their empire. A single arch could span a small river. To make longer bridges, Roman engineers built several arches end to end across rivers. Underwater supports kept the legs of the arches in the middle of a river from sinking into the soft mud of the river bottom. One of the most impressive Roman arched bridges is the Alcantara Bridge. It crosses the Tagus River in Spain. Built between A.D. 104 and 106, the bridge consists of six stone arches. The two center arches stand 157 feet (48 m) above the river below.

A BUILDING BREAKTHROUGH

A building material called pozzolana is named for its source, the Italian city of Pozzuoli. The reddish brown ash comes from volcanic eruptions. Roman

builders mixed pozzolana with crushed stone, lime, and other substances. The mixture created a totally new material—concrete. It was both strong and lightweight.

Concrete revolutionized building in ancient Rome. It made construction faster, easier, and cheaper. Roman workers could quickly pour concrete walls that would have taken years to build from brick.

To make concrete walls, builders first made hollow wooden forms, or molds. They filled the forms with wet concrete. After the concrete hardened, workers tore down the forms. This method allowed builders to create new architectural elements, including domes for roofs. The Pantheon, a famous temple in Rome, had a huge concrete dome. It measured 142 feet (43 m) across.

ANCIENT SUPERDOME

The Colosseum is a giant amphitheater, or stadium-style theater, in Rome. In modern times, the building is partially in ruins. But for almost two

Modern visitors tour the inside of the Colosseum, which seated fifty thousand people.

thousand years, it was the biggest amphitheater in the world. The oval structure was 620 feet (189 km) long, 513 feet (156 km) wide, and 157 feet (48 m) high. Its outer walls were made from a series of arches placed end to end.

Construction of the Colosseum began in A.D. 70 and continued for ten years. Builders used brick and concrete to make the walls. They covered the outside of the building with stone. Other ancient amphitheaters had to be dug into cliffs or hillsides, which supported the walls. But the Colosseum is freestanding. Its sturdy concrete and brick walls stand alone without outside support.

The Colosseum seated fifty thousand spectators. It was larger than some modern football stadiums. From its marble seats, spectators watched fights between gladiators (human fighters) and between gladiators and wild animals. Sometimes the Romans even flooded the Colosseum for mock battles between ships.

"I found a city of brick and left a city of marble."

—Roman Emperor Augustus, quoted by the Roman historian Suetonius, first or second century A.D.

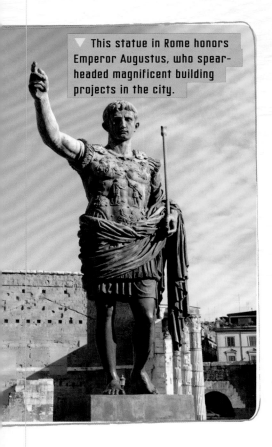

This statue in Rome honors Emperor Augustus, who spearheaded magnificent building projects in the city.

BIG CITY, BIG BUILDINGS

The city of Rome was the capital of the Roman Empire. At its peak in the first century A.D., it was home to one million people. This big city had tall apartment buildings. Some were six or seven stories high. The Roman poet Juvenal joked that people looking out the windows of tall buildings couldn't see carts on the streets below. Architects tried to outdo one another by creating taller and taller buildings.

The Roman emperor Augustus, who reigned from 27 B.C. to A.D. 14, wanted to make Rome a magnificent city. He wanted it to rival the splendor of ancient Greece. Augustus had many old buildings restored and ordered new ones to be created. The new buildings included the Temple of Mars Ultor, dedicated to Mars, the Roman god of war. It was built around A.D. 2. This imposing structure featured dozens of caryatids (columns carved in the shape of women). The temple also featured gleaming white marble inside and out.

160 NORTH STREET

Rome was not a planned city. It grew haphazardly. Its narrow streets and alleyways wind along the Tiber River and over the city's many hills. But when the Romans conquered new territory, they established towns according to a set plan.

They built two main streets, which crossed in the town center. The crossroads divided the town into four quarters. The main streets were usually named according to the points on a compass—north, south, east, and west.

Smaller streets led off the main streets. At the center of town, the Romans usually built a marketplace, an amphitheater, public baths, a temple, and an assembly hall. They built houses and apartment buildings on side streets. Towns usually included an army barracks. A surrounding wall helped protect residents from enemy attacks.

In *De Architectura*, Roman architect Vitruvius offered this advice on choosing the site for a new town:

> In setting out the walls of a city, choice of a healthy situation [site] is of the first importance; it should be on high ground, neither subject to fogs nor rains; its [weather] should be neither violently hot nor intensely cold, but temperate [moderate] in both respects. The neighborhood of a marshy place must be avoided.

LET THE SUN SHINE IN

Window glass was one of the greatest advances in construction technology. Imagine living in a home without windows. Many ancient peoples did. Imagine living in a home with windows but no window glass. People might cover the openings with curtains or shutters, but cold winds, insects, birds, rain, and snow still sometimes came through the windows.

Historians think the ancient Egyptians were the first glassmakers. They were making glass vessels by about 1500 B.C. The Phoenicians, based in modern-day Lebanon, were master glassmakers. They exported beautiful glass vases, bowls, and other objects around the Mediterranean world. The Phoenicians perfected the art of glassblowing. They learned to shape and manipulate melted glass by blowing on it through a tube. The first window glass was probably made from a bubble of blown glass opened into a flat sheet.

Roman glassmakers borrowed and improved upon the glassmaking technology of the Phoenicians. Before Roman glassmaking, only the rich could afford window glass. But as glassmaking became more widespread, glass became less expensive. By the first century A.D., window glass was common in many Roman towns. The cooler the weather, the more likely people were to have window glass.

The Romans probably made window glass by casting. They poured molten (melted) glass into smooth molds. Most windowpanes were about 12 by 24 inches (30 by 60 cm), although some were much bigger. One windowpane from the Roman city of Pompeii was 40 inches (102 cm) long, 28 inches (71 cm) wide, and a 0.5 inch (1.3 cm) thick.

BUILT TO LAST

By A.D. 117, the Roman Empire had reached its greatest size. It stretched from Great Britain in the north, south to northern Africa and Egypt, and east to the Tigris and Euphrates rivers of the Middle East. To connect parts of this vast empire, the Romans built 50,000 miles (80,000 km) of roads.

The oldest and most famous Roman road was the Via Appia, or Appian Way. Started in 312 B.C., this road led from Rome to the city of Tarentum, Italy. Builders later extended the road to the Adriatic Sea on Italy's eastern coast. The road was more than 350 miles (563 km) long and 35 feet (11 m) wide.

Roman roads were engineered to last. Each road had a sturdy foundation, up to 5 feet (1.5 m) thick. The foundation was made of layers of packed earth, stone blocks, broken stone, sand, and other materials. Workers paved the roads with blocks of cut stone.

Roads through rainy areas had cambered, or arched, surfaces. They were higher in the center than at the sides. This shape let rainwater drain off quickly, so it didn't soak in and damage the pavement. Most Roman roads also had curbstones and drainage ditches at the sides.

Roman roads remained the best in Europe for centuries, long after the fall of the Roman Empire. In modern times, parts of the Via Appia are still in use.

AQUEDUCTS

An aqueduct is a structure for carrying a large amount of flowing water. People in ancient Mesopotamia built the first aqueducts. The Romans were the ancient world's greatest aqueduct builders. Eleven aqueducts carried water from mountain streams and springs into the city of Rome. Engineers built other aqueducts throughout the Roman Empire.

The Pont du Gard in southern France was the tallest aqueduct in the Roman Empire. After the empire fell to invaders, people neglected the aqueducts. Their channels filled up with dirt.

Some Roman aqueducts were underground channels. Others were aboveground structures. They looked like long arched bridges. They had channels for carrying water on top. The tallest aqueduct in the Roman Empire is still standing. It is the Pont du Gard in Nimes, France. Built between A.D. 40 and 60, the structure stands 162 feet (49 m) high. It has three tiers of stone arches. It once carried water over the Gard River to the city of Nimes.

Aqueducts sloped slightly. That way, gravity pulled the water through the channels to its destination, with no need for pumps. Rome's aqueducts brought about 97 million gallons (367 million liters) of water to the city each day. The total system covered 260 miles (418 km). The water flowed into big distribution tanks. Then it traveled through pipes into buildings, fountains, toilets, and sewers.

PLUMBING AND HEATING

A few wealthy Romans had private bathrooms in their homes. But most ordinary Romans washed at public bathhouses and used public toilets.

Public restrooms contained fifteen or twenty square stone toilets, lined up against walls. A drainage system beneath the toilets carried waste into city sewers. Romans customarily chatted with one another in public toilets. They did not find this lack of privacy embarrassing.

Romans also socialized at public baths. The baths were community centers as well as recreation areas. They had facilities you might find in a modern-day spa, such as swimming pools, steam rooms, and gymnasiums. In addition, Roman baths had gardens, dining rooms, libraries, meeting rooms, and other facilities.

The Romans built baths all over their empire. The Baths of Hadrian in modern-day Libya, in North Africa, were constructed of green, pink, black, and white marble. The baths in Aquae Sulis, England (the modern-day city of Bath), were fed by an underground hot spring. The baths at Caracalla, Italy, were some of the most impressive. They were filled with marble seats,

fountains, and statues. Beautiful mosaics (images made from small pieces of glass or stone) adorned the floors and walls. Water for the baths came from the Aqua Marcia aqueduct. The Baths of Diocletian, in the city of Rome, were the largest baths in the empire. They covered more than 32 acres (13 hectares). Three thousand people could use the facilities at one time.

The Romans heated public baths, homes, and other buildings with hypocausts. These were the same kind of central heating systems as those of ancient China. Like the Chinese, the Romans built floors on stone pillars. They left a hollow area beneath the

◄ Roman baths had public toilets, like this one near Lebda, Libya. The round toilet seats are in the foreground.

▼ The once-magnificent baths of Caracalla, Italy, have fallen into ruin.

This Roman bathhouse in Spain was heated with a hypocaust system. Warm air from a furnace circulated around the stone posts. The posts were covered with flooring in ancient times. The warm air beneath the floor warmed the room *(above)*.

floor and ground of each room. Hot air from a furnace circulated under the floors. The circulating air warmed rooms before escaping through a pipe in the roof. The furnace usually burned charcoal or wood. Unlike fireplaces, which heated just one room, hypocausts provided steady warmth throughout entire dwellings.

TUNNELS

From A.D. 41 to 52, Roman builders undertook a great feat of engineering. They dug a 3.5-mile (5.6 km) underground tunnel. The tunnel drained water from Lake Fucinus in central Italy and channeled it into a nearby river. Once the lake was drained, Romans used the dry lake bed for farmland. To create the tunnel, workers dug shafts about 120 feet (37 m) apart and 400 feet (122 m) deep. They climbed down ladders to the bottom of each shaft. Then they dug sideways, connecting the tunnel from one shaft to the next. It took thirty thousand workers ten years to build the tunnel.

How did the ancient Romans tunnel through rock without drills and other power tools? Actually, Roman tunnel builders usually didn't dig rock, they burned it. They used a technique called fire quenching. They heated the rock with fire and then cooled it quickly with water. The fast cooling process caused the rock to crack. Once the rock cracked, workers could remove it easily. They hauled away the rock, built another fire, and kept up the process as a tunnel grew foot by foot.

Roman builders preferred to build tunnels in very hard rock. The hard rock supported the walls of the tunnel. That way, workers didn't need to line tunnels with brick or stone.

AFTER THE ANCIENTS

Ancient civilizations rose and fell. Often civilizations grew politically or economically weak and stronger groups conquered them. But even after a civilization died out, its technology often remained. Conquering groups built on the knowledge of conquered peoples to further develop technology.

This wasn't always the case, however. After the Roman Empire fell to invaders in A.D. 476, Europe entered a period called the Middle Ages (about 500–1500). The early Middle Ages are sometimes called the Dark Ages, because art, culture, and learning did not flourish in Europe during these years. Few people in Europe went to school. Few craftspeople knew about or improved upon ancient technology.

REBIRTH

In the 1300s, Europeans took a renewed interest in learning, literature, art, and technology, including architecture. Europe entered a period of creative outpouring called the Renaissance (1300s–1600). The name *Renaissance* means "rebirth."

Not only did Europeans explore brand-new ideas in art and culture during the Renaissance, they also looked to ancient Greece and Rome for inspiration. In the 1400s, Italian scholars discovered and reprinted Vitruvius's *De Architectura*. European architects used the old book as a guide. They built structures using domes, vaults, Corinthian columns, and other features straight out of ancient Greece and Rome. *De Architectura* was the most important book of its kind for hundreds of years. European architects during the following centuries included many of its ideas in their own books on architecture.

NEOCLASSICISM

In the mid-1700s, archaeologists rediscovered the ancient Roman cities of Pompeii and Herculaneum. The cities had been buried for more than one thousand years beneath a thick layer of volcanic ash. The eruption of Mount Vesuvius had destroyed the cities in A.D. 79. When archaeologists began to excavate the cities, they set off a new wave of interest in Roman architecture. European architects copied designs of buildings uncovered by the excavations.

▼ The discovery of the ruins of Pompeii in Italy kicked off an era of new interest in ancient architecture.

Architects took a renewed interest in ancient Greek buildings as well. They worked in a new building style called neoclassical. *Neo* means "new," and *classical* refers to the culture and art of ancient Greece and Rome. In copying ancient designs, neoclassical architects reproduced ancient styles much more closely than architects of the Renaissance had done.

Neoclassicism began in Europe but soon moved to the United States. U.S. architect Henry Bacon loved the Parthenon and other classical buildings. He studied the Parthenon carefully. He used it as a model for his most famous structure, the Lincoln Memorial in Washington, D.C. The memorial was built between 1915 and 1922.

▼ The Lincoln Memorial in Washington, D.C., is modeled on the Parthenon in Athens, Greece. Other U.S. and European buildings also copy classical styles.

The walls of this house in New Mexico were made with adobe, an ancient building material. Inside, the house has modern plumbing and heating systems.

OLD AND NEW

Ancient construction has never really left us. In some places, modern people live in the same kinds of houses used by their ancestors hundreds or thousands of years ago. In the deserts of North Africa, some nomads (traveling people) still build simple tents made from cloth and a frame of poles. In parts of South America, people still build houses from reeds, poles, and thatch. People still live in mud brick houses in many parts of the world. Some of these houses are old structures built generations ago, but many are brand new. In the Southeast Asian nation of Malaysia and in other wet places, people still build houses on stilts. They make the walls from wood and bamboo and the roofs from thatch. Often people combine ancient and modern building materials. For instance, in the U.S. state of New Mexico, you might see an old adobe house with modern factory-made doors and windows.

In recent years, many modern builders have discovered what ancient people already knew: houses made from simple, natural materials can be inexpensive and energy efficient. Modern homeowners have found that by building a house partially underground or against a hillside, they can cut down on heating and cooling bills. That's because the earth makes great insulation. In some parts of the United States, you might see modern people living in yurts. These ancient houses originated in the deserts of central Asia. Herders used them as temporary shelters when they traveled across the deserts with their animals. Traditional yurts were made of a frame of poles with a covering of felt, or matted woolen fibers. The houses were easily disassembled, transported, and rebuilt in new locations. Many modern yurt dwellers like the homes for their simplicity, low cost, and ease of construction. They also feel more connected to nature in a yurt than they do in a modern-style home.

▼ Some modern Mongolian herders use yurts as temporary shelters. This yurt is in the Gorkhi-Terelj National Park in Mongolia.

Archaeologists began unearthing the Theater of Epidaurus in 1881. Modern actors perform ancient Greek plays in this theater, which lies in modern-day Greece.

STILL GOING STRONG

At the Theater of Epidaurus in Greece, modern visitors can take a trip back in time. Sitting on the theater's stadium-style limestone seating, they can imagine what it might have been like to view a show there in 350 B.C., when the place was brand new. The theater was part of a religious sanctuary (retreat) dedicated to Asclepius, the Greek god of healing. In addition to the theater, the sanctuary held a temple, a sports arena, and a public bath.

Ancient Greeks came to the theater to see works by Aeschylus, Sophocles, and Aristophanes—some of the greatest playwrights of the ancient world. People also came to hear music and poetry contests. Built against a hillside, the giant, semicircular stadium could hold thirteen thousand theatergoers. Performers stood on a round central stage. A small building stood behind the stage. It provided a theatrical backdrop for the plays and other performances.

Greek people used the theater for more than one thousand years. Eventually, though, it was abandoned. Winds blew dirt over the seats and the stage. Rainstorms filled the stadium with more dirt and mud. Plants grew over the newly deposited layers of earth. Finally, the stadium was completely buried and forgotten.

Then, in 1881, a Greek archaeologist began to unearth the stadium. Excavations continued on and off for many years. Archaeologists found that the stage building had fallen down, but the stage and the seats seemed as good as new. Excavators were pleased to discover that the theater had excellent acoustics, or the ability to transmit sound. When they dropped a coin on the stage, people in the top row of seats could hear it.

To twentieth-century Greeks, the next step seemed only natural. In 1954 they began staging ancient Greek dramas at the theater. These plays have continued into the twenty-first century. Every summer, thousands of visitors arrive for the Epidaurus Festival. They watch classic Greek dramas and can feel themselves transported back in time.

TIMELINE

CA. 10,000 B.C.	People in the ancient Middle East begin to settle into villages.
CA. 6000 B.C.	People in Mesopotamia begin to build with sun-dried bricks.
CA. 3500 B.C.	Mesopotamians begin to fire clay bricks in ovens.
CA. 2900 B.C.	Egyptians build a dam on a river southwest of Cairo.
CA. 2800 TO 1500 B.C.	People in Great Britain build Stonehenge.
CA. 2650 B.C.	Egyptian workers build the Step Pyramid at Saqqara near the Nile River.
CA. 2600–2500 B.C.	Egyptian workers build the Great Pyramid at Giza.
CA. 2400 B.C.	Indus Valley people build a dock at Lothal.
CA. 2180–2160 B.C.	Workers build a brick-lined tunnel beneath the Euphrates River in Babylon.
CA. 2100 B.C.	Workers build the Ziggurat of Ur.
605–562 B.C.	Nebuchadrezzar II rules the Babylonian kingdom. He builds brick walls around the city of Babylon and builds the Hanging Gardens of Babylon.
500s B.C.	Workers build the Etemenanki ziggurat, which might have inspired the biblical story of the Tower of Babel. Workers build the Temple of Artemis at Ephesus in modern-day Turkey.
447–432 B.C.	Ancient Greeks build the Parthenon.
CA. 430 B.C.	Phidias creates the Statue of Zeus at Olympia.
CA. 350 B.C.	Ancient Greeks build the Theater of Epidaurus.
331 B.C.	The Macedonian general Alexander the Great founds the city of Alexandria, Egypt.
312 B.C.	Workers begin construction on the Appian Way in Rome.
294–282 B.C.	Greek workers build the Colossus of Rhodes.
283–246 B.C.	Workers build the Pharos of Alexandria.
200s B.C.	Building begins on the Great Wall of China.
27 B.C.	Roman architect Marcus Vitruvius writes *De Architectura*.
A.D. 2	Emperor Augustus builds the Temple of Mars Ultor in Rome.

40–60	Romans build the Pont du Gard, an aqueduct in southern France.
41–52	Romans build a tunnel to drain Lake Fucinus in central Italy.
70–80	Roman workers build the Colosseum in Rome.
104–106	Romans build the Alcantara Bridge in Spain.
312	Roman emperor Constantine builds an arch in Rome to honor his victory in battle.
476	The Roman Empire falls to invaders.
1200s	People in the Four Corners area of the southwestern United States build cliff houses at Mesa Verde.
1300s	Europe enters an era called the Renaissance, a time of renewed interest in learning, art, and culture. Earthquakes damage the Pharos in Alexandria.
1400s	Italian scholars discover and reprint Vitruvius's *De Architectura.* The Inca build Machu Picchu, a royal estate in Peru.
1400 TO 1600	Easter Islanders carve almost nine hundred statues called moai.
1500s	European explorers arrive in the Western Hemisphere.
MID-1700s	Archaeologists begin to excavate the Roman cities of Pompeii and Herculaneum, which had been buried by eruptions of Mount Vesuvius in A.D. 79. European architects begin to work in the neoclassical style.
1881	Archaeologists begin to excavate the Theater of Epidaurus.
1915–1922	Workers build the Lincoln Memorial in Washington, D.C., whose design is based on the Parthenon in Athens, Greece.
1921	Archaeologists begin excavating the Indus Valley sites of Harappa and Mohenjo Daro.
1954	People begin staging ancient Greek dramas at the Theater of Epidaurus.
2001	Archaeologists date Caral, Peru, to 2600 B.C. and determine that it is the oldest town in the Western Hemisphere.
2002–2003	Archaeologists find burials at Stonehenge dating to around 2500 B.C.
2010	Archaeologists find a twenty-three-thousand-year-old stone wall in the Theopetra Cave in Greece.

GLOSSARY

ACOUSTICS: the ability to transmit sound for distinct hearing

ACROPOLIS: a fortified section of an ancient Greek city, containing temples and government buildings and located on a hill

ADOBE: bricks made of sun-dried earth and straw

AQUEDUCT: a canal, a pipe, or a bridgelike structure used to carry a large amount of flowing water

ARCH: a curved architectural structure used to span an opening, such as a doorway

ARCHAEOLOGIST: a scientist who studies the remains of past human cultures

ARCHITECTURE: the art and science of designing and building structures

ARTIFACT: a human-made object, especially one characteristic of a certain group or historical period

BATHHOUSE: a building with facilities for swimming and bathing

BITUMEN: a by-product of petroleum, used as mortar in ancient times

COLUMN: a pillar that supports a roof or a ceiling

CONCRETE: a hard, strong building material made by mixing minerals with water

CORBELED ROOF: a roof made of layers of stones or other material. Each layer projects farther into the interior of the building than the one beneath it, until the two sides of the roof meet.

DOME: a large hemispherical (resembling half a ball) roof or ceiling

GLAZE: a hard, glassy outer coating on fired pottery or bricks

HUNTER-GATHERERS: people who obtain their food by hunting, fishing, and gathering wild plants

INSULATION: any material that blocks the flow of heat, keeping warm air and cold air separate

MONUMENT: a stone or structure built to honor a person or event

MORTAR: a substance such as cement that seals the spaces between brick, stone, or other building materials

PIT HOUSE: a house built partially underground, so that the earth forms the lower part of the house walls

PYRAMID: a massive structure with a square base and triangular walls that meet at a point at the top

RADIOCARBON DATING: a method for determining the age of a once-living thing by measuring and comparing the amount of radiocarbon and nitrogen it contains

TERRACE: a series of ledges cut into a hillside or a raised mound of earth. People often create terraces to farm hilly countryside.

THATCH: a mat of straw or other plant material used as a roof

TIER: a level or a layer

VAULT: an arched roof that resembles a half barrel or a half tunnel

WATTLE AND DAUB: a method of building homes using a framework of poles or reeds covered by mud

SOURCE NOTES

17   Dan Fletcher, "Stonehenge Theories," Time.com, March 20, 2009, http://www.time.com/time/world/article/0,8599,1886661,00.html (April 22, 2010).

23   Herodotus, *Herodotus*, bk. 1 and 2, trans. A. D. Godley (London: William Heinemann, 1920), 223.

30   Ida Pfeiffer, "A Visit to the Holy Land, Egypt and Italy," Project Gutenberg, 2004, http://www.gutenberg.org/files/12561/12561.txt (April 22, 2010).

36   Charles Masson, "Narrative of Various Journeys in Balochistan, Afghanistan, and the Panjab," Harappa.com, 1996, http://www.harappa.com/har/masson0.html (April 22, 2010).

44   John Barrow, "Travels in China," Project Gutenberg, 2009, http://www.gutenberg.org/files/28729/28729-8.txt (April 11, 2010).

53   Kim MacQuarrie, *The Last Days of the Incas* (New York: Simon and Schuster, 2007), 385.

56   Visit Ancient Greece, "A Guide for Tourists: Visit Ancient Greece," Visit-ancient-greece.com, 2009, http://www.visit-ancient-greece.com/ (April 22, 2010).

62–63 Peter A. Clayton, and Martin Price, eds. *The Seven Wonders of the Ancient World* (London: Routledge, 1988), 66.

63   Ian Chilvers, *Oxford Dictionary of Art* (Oxford: Oxford University Press, 2004), 162.

65   Hugh Honour and John Fleming, *A World History of Art* (London: Laurence King Publishing, 2005), 185.

69   Fik Meijer, *Emperors Don't Die in Bed* (New York: Routledge, 2001), 17.

71   Appleton, *Appleton's Annual Cyclopaedia and Register of Important Events of the Year 1880*, vol. 5 (New York: D. Appleton and Company, 1887), 358.

SELECTED BIBLIOGRAPHY

Adkins, Lesley, and Roy A. Adkins. *Handbook to Life in Ancient Rome*. New York: Facts on File, 1994.

Clark, Ronald W. *Works of Man*. New York: Viking, 1985.

Courtenay-Thompson, Fiona, Roger Tritton, and Nicola Liddiard, eds. *The Visual Dictionary of Buildings*. London: Dorling Kindersley, 1992.

Cox, Reg, and Neil Morris. *The Seven Wonders of the Ancient World*. Parsippany, NJ: Silver Burdett Press, 1996.

Fagan, Brian M., ed. *Discovery: Unearthing the New Treasures of Archaeology*. London: Thames and Hudson, 2007.

——. *The Seventy Great Inventions of the Ancient World*. London: Thames and Hudson, 2004.

Feuerstein, Georg, Subhash Kak, and David Frawley. *In Search of the Cradle of Civilization*. Wheaton, IL: Theosophical Publishing House, 1995.

Glancey, Jonathan. *Architecture*. New York: DK Publishing, 2006.

Ingpen, Robert, and Philip Wilkinson. *Encyclopedia of Ideas That Changed the World*. New York: Penguin Books, 1993.

James, Peter, and Nick Thorpe. *Ancient Inventions*. New York: Ballantine Books, 1994.

Oates, David, and Joan Oates. *The Rise of Civilization*. New York: Elsevier Phaidon, 1976.

Oliver, Paul. *Dwellings: The Vernacular House World Wide*. New York: Phaidon Press, 2003.

Raeburn, Michael. *Architecture of the World*. New York: Galahad Books, 1975.

Saggs, H. W. F. *Civilization before Greece and Rome*. New Haven, CT: Yale University Press, 1989.

Stevenson, Neil. *Architecture*. New York: Dorling Kindersley, 1997.

White, K. D. *Greek and Roman Technology*. Ithaca, NY: Cornell University Press, 1984.

FURTHER READING

Arnold, Caroline. *The Ancient Cliff Dwellers of Mesa Verde*. New York: Sandpiper, 2000.
    Accompanied by beautiful color photographs, this book explores the ancient cliff dwellings in Mesa Verde, Colorado. Author Caroline Arnold describes the Ancestral Puebloan people who lived there, as well as modern archaeological excavations.

Behnke, Alison. *The Conquests of Alexander the Great*. Minneapolis: Twenty-First Century Books, 2008.
    Alexander the Great founded the famous city of Alexandria, Egypt, home to the Pharos and other impressive ancient structures. This book describes his life and achievements.

Du Temple, Lesley. *The Colosseum*. Minneapolis: Twenty-First Century Books, 2003.
    This book examines one of the greatest works of ancient construction, the Colosseum in Rome. Readers will learn how the giant stadium was built and what went on inside it.

———. *The Great Wall of China*. Minneapolis: Twenty-First Century Books, 2003.
    The Great Wall of China is one of the most impressive feats of ancient construction. This book tells the story of the wall from ancient to modern times.

Kirkpatrick, Naida. *The Indus Valley*. Chicago: Heinemann Library, 2002.
The ancient Indus Valley people created some of the world's first planned towns. This book examines Indus Valley cities and the artifacts.

Passport to History series. Minneapolis: Twenty-First Century Books, 2001–2004.
In this series, readers will take trips back in time to ancient China, Egypt, Greece, Rome, and the Mayan civilization. They will learn about people's clothing, work, buildings, and other aspects of daily life.

Perl, Lila. *The Ancient Maya*. New York: Franklin Watts, 2005.
Ancient Mayan cities included fabulous stepped pyramids. This title examines Mayan life and culture.

Unearthing Ancient Worlds series. Minneapolis: Twenty-First Century Books, 2008–2009.
This series takes readers on journeys of discovery, as archaeologists discover the mysterious moai of Easter Island, the royal Inca city of Machu Picchu, the ruins of Pompeii, and other archaeological treasures.

Visual Geography Series. Minneapolis: Twenty-First Century Books, 2003–2011.
Each book in this series examines one country, with lots of information about its ancient history, customs, geography, and economy. The series' companion website, Vgsbooks.com, offers free, downloadable material and links to sites with additional information about each country.

Woods, Michael, and Mary B. Woods. Seven Wonders of the Ancient World series. Minneapolis: Twenty-First Century Books, 2009.
This series explores Herodotus's list of the seven ancient wonders as well as magnificent buildings and monuments from ancient Africa, Asia, Central and South America, and North America.

WEBSITES

EXPLORE THE PYRAMIDS

http://www.nationalgeographic.com/pyramids/pyramids.html
> This website from *National Geographic* magazine offers a detailed guide to Egyptian pyramids.

IGLOO CONSTRUCTION TIPS

> http://www.igloomag.com/newswire::78::Igloo_Construction_Tips
> If you live in a snowy place, you can build your own igloo. This Web page tells you how.

MESA VERDE

> http://www.nps.gov/meve/index.htm
> This website from the U.S. National Park Service introduces the people who built the ancient cliff dwellings at Mesa Verde, describes the modern-day national park, and offers special links for kids.

ROMAN BATH

> http://www.pbs.org/wgbh/nova/lostempires/roman/
> This website is a companion to the NOVA television film *Roman Bath*, part of the Secrets of Lost Empires series. This site takes visitors on a tour of a typical Roman bath. It also explores the aqueducts that brought water to cities in the Roman Empire.

INDEX

ABOUT THE AUTHORS

Michael Woods is a science and medical journalist in Washington, D.C. He has won many national writing awards. Mary B. Woods is a school librarian. Their past books include the fifteen-volume Disasters Up Close series, the seven-volume 7 Wonders of the Ancient World series, and the seven-volume 7 Wonders of the Natural World series. The Woodses have four children. When not writing, reading, or enjoying their grandchildren, the Woodses travel to gather material for future books.

PHOTO ACKNOWLEDGMENTS

The images in this book are used with the permission of: © Igorr/Dreamstime.com (all backgrounds); © Hemis.fr/SuperStock, pp. 3, 8, 46-47; © Laura Westlund/Independent Picture Service, pp. 4-5; © Yoshio Tomii/SuperStock, pp. 6, 54; © RIA Novosti/Photo Researchers, Inc., p. 10; Library of Congress, p. 12 (LC-USZ62-135985); © William McFarlane/George Eastman House/Archive Photos/Getty Images, p. 13; © Peter Marble/Dreamstime.com, p. 15; © Robert Harding Picture Library/SuperStock, pp. 16, 25, 37, 59, 68, 79; © Silvio Fiore/SuperStock, pp. 18, 27; © Mesopotamian/The Bridgeman Art Library/Getty Images, p. 20; © Paul Rapson/Photo Researchers, Inc., p. 21; © North Wind Picture Archives, p. 24; © Diademimages/Dreamstime.com, pp. 28-29; AP Photo/Tim Roske, p. 29; © Frans Lemmens/SuperStock, p. 30; © Science & Society Picture Library/Getty Images, p. 31; © Kenneth Garrett/Danita Delimont/Alamy, p. 33; © Paolo Koch/Photo Researchers, Inc., pp. 34-35; © age fotostock/SuperStock, pp. 38, 46, 51, 66, 67; © Dr. Pramod Bansode/Dreamstime.com, p. 39; © Ashley Cooper/Visuals Unlimited, Inc./Getty Images, pp. 40-41; © Topham/The Image Works, p. 41; © Dennis Cox/ChinaStock, p. 42; © Lambert (Bart) Parren/Dreamstime.com, p. 43; © Tim Hall/Axiom Photographic Agency/Getty Images, p. 44; © Stock Connection/SuperStock, p. 45; © Dmitry Rukhlenko/Dreamstime.com, p. 48; © DEA/G. Dagli Orti/De Agostini/Getty Images, p. 49; © Prisma/SuperStock, pp. 52, 56-57; © James Brunker/Alamy, p. 55; © Edmund Nagele PCL/SuperStock, p. 57; © Index Stock/SuperStock, p. 58; © Lonely Planet/SuperStock, p. 60; © SuperStock/SuperStock, pp. 61, 62, 63; © imagebroker.net/SuperStock, pp. 64-65; © Hidekazu Nishibata/SuperStock, p. 65; © Louise Parry/Dreamstime.com, pp. 68-69; © Brancaleone/Dreamstime.com, p. 70; © Wessel Cirkel/Dreamstime.com, p. 73; © Joseph Eid/AFP/Getty Images, p. 75 (top); © Veronica Giu/Dreamstime.com, p. 75 (bottom); © Travel Ink/Gallo Images/Getty Images, p. 76; © David Kovziridze/Dreamstime.com, p. 80; © Morey Milbradt/Brand X Pictures/Getty Images, p. 81; © John F. White/SuperStock, p. 82; © Erin Babnik/Alamy, p. 83.

Front cover: © Tenback/Dreamstime.com (top left); © Astra490/Dreamstime.com (top right); © iStockphoto.com/Jouke van der Meer (bottom); © Igorr/Dreamstime.com (background).

Back cover: © Igorr/Dreamstime.com (background).